Mastering Bootstrap 5: From Basics to Expert Projects

Kameron Hussain and Frahaan Hussain

Published by Sonar Publishing, 2023.

MASTERING BOOTSTRAP 5: FROM BASICS TO EXPERT PROJECTS

First edition. December 9, 2023.

ISBN: 979-8223618362

Written by Kameron Hussain and Frahaan Hussain.

Table of Contents

Update Dependencies

Test and Debug

Plan for Compatibility

Explore New Features

Consider Performance

Plan Training and Education

Engage with the Community

20.5 Continuing Education and Resources

Lifelong Learning

Online Courses and Tutorials

Documentation and Official Resources

Books and Ebooks

Web Development Blogs

Webinars and Conferences

Online Communities and Forums

GitHub Repositories

Code Challenges and Practice

Online Design and Development Tools

Professional Networking

Chapter 1: Introduction to Bootstrap 5

1.1. Understanding Bootstrap 5: Evolution and Features

Bootstrap, initially released in 2011, has become one of the most popular front-end frameworks for web development. With its latest iteration, Bootstrap 5, this open-source toolkit continues to evolve, offering new features and enhancements that make building responsive, mobile-first websites more accessible and efficient.

The most notable change in Bootstrap 5 is the dropping of jQuery as a dependency. This shift represents a significant move towards modern JavaScript standards, as jQuery's necessity has diminished with the advancements in vanilla JavaScript and ECMAScript standards.

Removal of jQuery Dependency

In previous versions, Bootstrap relied heavily on jQuery for its JavaScript components. However, Bootstrap 5 has rewritten all its components in vanilla JavaScript, making the framework lighter and faster. This change not only reduces the overall project file size but also improves performance, as native JavaScript tends to be faster than jQuery-based code.

Enhanced Grid System

Bootstrap 5 introduces an updated grid system, which is more flexible and extendable. The new grid system offers more customization options, allowing developers to create more complex and responsive layouts. It includes additional classes for gutter spacing, column wrapping, order classes, and more.

Improved Customization

Customization in Bootstrap 5 is more straightforward, thanks to the increased use of CSS custom properties (variables). These variables make it easier to theme and adjust the styling of Bootstrap components without delving deep into the source code.

Updated Form Controls

Bootstrap 5 brings a fresh look to form controls with improved styling and better consistency across browsers. This update includes new styles for checkboxes, radio buttons, switches, file inputs, and select menus, ensuring a more uniform appearance across different platforms.

Enhanced Navbars

The navbar component, a staple in website navigation, has been improved in Bootstrap 5. The new navbar is more flexible, with enhanced support for different types of content, better responsiveness, and easier customization.

New and Updated Components

Bootstrap 5 introduces new components and updates existing ones. Notable additions include offcanvas menus, accordion widgets, and floating labels for form fields. These new components provide more options for interactive and modern web design.

Focus on Accessibility

Accessibility has always been a priority for Bootstrap, and version 5 continues this trend. The new release includes various improvements to make websites more accessible, such as better form control feedback and updated contrast ratios for better visibility.

Responsive Font Sizes

Another significant addition is the responsive font sizes feature. This feature automatically adjusts font sizes based on the viewport size, making it easier to create readable text on different devices without writing extensive media queries.

Utility API

Bootstrap 5 introduces a Utility API, allowing developers to create their own utility classes. This feature enables greater flexibility in extending the framework to suit specific design needs.

Conclusion

Bootstrap 5 marks a significant step forward in the framework's evolution. Its focus on modern JavaScript, enhanced customization, improved components, and commitment to accessibility make it a solid choice for web developers looking to build responsive and engaging websites.

With these advancements, Bootstrap 5 sets the stage for even more innovative web design and development, maintaining its position as a leading front-end framework in the industry. As the web continues to evolve, Bootstrap is poised to evolve with it, offering tools and features that meet the needs of modern web development.

1.2. Setting Up the Development Environment

Setting up the development environment for Bootstrap 5 involves a few key steps to ensure a smooth workflow. This process includes installing necessary tools, setting up a project structure, and understanding the basics of integrating Bootstrap into your web project.

Installing Node.js and npm

The first step is to install Node.js, which comes with npm (Node Package Manager). npm is essential for managing dependencies, including Bootstrap and its associated tools. To install Node.js, visit Node.js official website[1] and download the installer for your operating system.

After installing, you can verify the installation by running the following commands in your terminal or command prompt:

node -v

npm -v

These commands will display the installed versions of Node.js and npm, respectively.

Setting Up a Bootstrap Project

With Node.js and npm installed, you can now set up a Bootstrap project. Create a new directory for your project and navigate into it using the terminal. Then, initialize a new npm project:

npm init -y

This command creates a package.json file with default values.

Installing Bootstrap

To install Bootstrap, run the following command in your project directory:

---

1. https://nodejs.org/

```
npm install bootstrap@5
```

This command will install Bootstrap 5 and add it as a dependency in your package.json file.

Including Bootstrap in Your Project

There are several ways to include Bootstrap in your project. The simplest is to reference the Bootstrap CSS and JS files in your HTML.

You can link to the Bootstrap CDN:

```
<!—Bootstrap CSS—>

<link href="https://stackpath.bootstrapcdn.com/bootstrap/5.0.0-alpha1/css/bootstrap.min.css" rel="stylesheet">

<!—Optional JavaScript—>

<!—jQuery first, then Popper.js, then Bootstrap JS—>

<script src="https://code.jquery.com/jquery-3.5.1.slim.min.js"></script>

<script src="https://cdn.jsdelivr.net/npm/@popperjs/core@2.0.4/dist/umd/popper.min.js"></script>

<script src="https://stackpath.bootstrapcdn.com/bootstrap/5.0.0-alpha1/js/bootstrap.min.js"></script>
```

Or, if you installed Bootstrap via npm, you can include it from your node_modules:

```
<link href="node_modules/bootstrap/dist/css/bootstrap.min.css" rel="stylesheet">
```

```
<script src="node_modules/bootstrap/dist/js/bootstrap.bundle.min.js"></script>
```

Project Structure

Organize your project by creating a directory structure. A typical structure might look like this:

- index.html - your main HTML file.
- css/ - directory for custom CSS styles.
- js/ - directory for custom JavaScript files.
- node_modules/ - contains all npm dependencies, including Bootstrap.
- package.json - npm configuration file.

Customizing Bootstrap

If you want to customize Bootstrap's default styles, create a custom CSS file:

```
/* custom.css */

body {

background-color: #f8f9fa;

}
```

Include this file in your HTML after the Bootstrap CSS link:

```
<link href="node_modules/bootstrap/dist/css/bootstrap.min.css" rel="stylesheet">

<link href="css/custom.css" rel="stylesheet">
```

Using Bootstrap Components

Bootstrap comes with a variety of pre-designed components. To use them, simply add the appropriate Bootstrap classes to your HTML elements. For example, to create a Bootstrap button:

```
<button type="button" class="btn btn-primary">Primary Button</button>
```

Responsive Layouts

Bootstrap's grid system helps in creating responsive layouts. Use container, row, and column classes to structure your layout. For example:

```
<div class="container">

<div class="row">

<div class="col">

Column 1

</div>

<div class="col">

Column 2

</div>

</div>

</div>
```

JavaScript Components

Many Bootstrap components, like modals and carousels, require JavaScript. If you're using the Bootstrap bundle (as shown in the CDN example), it includes Popper.js and Bootstrap's JavaScript plugins.

Testing Your Setup

Create a simple Bootstrap page to test your setup. Include a navbar, a few buttons, and a grid layout. Check if everything displays correctly and responds to different screen sizes.

Conclusion

Setting up a development environment for Bootstrap 5 is straightforward. With Node.js and npm, you can easily manage Bootstrap and other dependencies. By following the steps above, you will have a solid foundation to start building responsive and modern web applications with Bootstrap 5.

1.3. Bootstrap 5 vs Previous Versions: What's New

Bootstrap 5 brings a plethora of changes and improvements over its predecessors, marking a significant shift in the framework's evolution. This section explores the key differences between Bootstrap 5 and previous versions, highlighting the updates and new features that set it apart.

Dropping jQuery Dependency

One of the most notable changes in Bootstrap 5 is the removal of jQuery as a dependency. Earlier versions relied on jQuery for

JavaScript components, but Bootstrap 5 has moved to vanilla JavaScript. This change leads to a lighter and faster framework, aligning with modern web development practices.

Updated Grid System

Bootstrap 5 introduces an enhanced grid system with more flexibility. It offers more customization options, such as gutter classes and updated utility classes, allowing for more sophisticated layouts.

New Components and Utilities

Bootstrap 5 adds several new components and utilities, enriching the toolkit for developers. New additions include offcanvas menus, avatars, and utility APIs that provide more control over the framework's inbuilt styles and functionalities.

Enhanced Customization with CSS Variables

Bootstrap 5 utilizes CSS custom properties (variables) extensively, enabling easier theming and customization. This approach allows for more dynamic styling and simplifies the process of overriding default styles.

Improved Navbar

The navbar component in Bootstrap 5 has been revamped for greater flexibility and ease of use. It supports more customization options, better responsiveness, and accommodates various types of content more efficiently.

SVG Icons

Bootstrap 5 introduces a new SVG icon library, providing a wide range of icons that are easy to use and customize. This addition replaces the need for external icon libraries.

Enhanced Form Controls

Form controls in Bootstrap 5 have been redesigned for better consistency and appearance. This includes new styles for checkboxes, radio buttons, and switches, offering a more unified look across different browsers and platforms.

RTL Support

Right-to-left (RTL) support is a significant addition in Bootstrap 5, catering to languages that use RTL scripts. This feature ensures that Bootstrap-based websites are more accessible and inclusive globally.

Improved Accessibility

Accessibility has been a focus in Bootstrap 5, with improvements to ensure that websites are usable by everyone. This includes better keyboard navigation, screen reader support, and focus management.

Changes in JavaScript Components

With the shift to vanilla JavaScript, Bootstrap 5's JavaScript components have been rewritten, resulting in more efficient and streamlined code. This change enhances performance and reduces dependencies.

Dropped Internet Explorer Support

Bootstrap 5 has dropped support for Internet Explorer, aligning with modern browser standards and capabilities. This move allows for the use of newer CSS features and optimizations that are not compatible with older browsers.

Enhanced Documentation

The documentation for Bootstrap 5 has been overhauled, making it more comprehensive and user-friendly. It includes detailed guides, examples, and explanations, making it easier for new users to get started and for experienced users to find advanced information.

Modularity and Custom Builds

Bootstrap 5 emphasizes modularity, allowing developers to pick and choose the components they need. This approach leads to lighter builds, especially beneficial for projects that require only specific parts of the framework.

Performance Improvements

Performance optimization is a key focus in Bootstrap 5. The use of vanilla JavaScript, CSS variables, and other modern techniques contribute to faster load times and smoother interactions.

Migration Ease

For projects upgrading from previous versions, Bootstrap 5 offers a migration guide. This guide provides detailed instructions and tips for a smooth transition, addressing breaking changes and deprecated features.

Conclusion

Bootstrap 5 represents a significant step forward in the framework's development, focusing on modern web standards, performance, and user experience. Its new features and improvements offer developers more tools and flexibility, making it an excellent choice for building responsive and accessible web applications. As the web continues to evolve, Bootstrap 5 is well-positioned to adapt and grow, remaining a cornerstone in the world of web development.

1.4. Core Concepts of Responsive Design

Responsive web design is a crucial aspect of modern web development, ensuring that websites look and function well on a variety of devices and screen sizes. Bootstrap 5, with its responsive design features, plays a pivotal role in achieving this adaptability. This section delves into the core concepts of responsive design as implemented in Bootstrap 5.

Mobile-First Approach

Bootstrap 5 adopts a mobile-first approach, meaning styles are designed for smaller screens first and then scaled up for larger screens. This approach is beneficial for performance, as it typically results in lighter styles for mobile devices.

The Grid System

The grid system is a foundational element of responsive design in Bootstrap. It uses a series of containers, rows, and columns to layout and align content. The grid is based on a 12-column structure, allowing for a variety of layouts. For example:

```
<div class="container">
```

```
<div class="row">
<div class="col-sm-6">Column 1</div>
<div class="col-sm-6">Column 2</div>
</div>
</div>
```

In this code, col-sm-6 creates two equal columns for small-sized screens and above.

Breakpoints

Breakpoints are predefined widths that determine how the layout responds to different screen sizes. Bootstrap 5 has five breakpoints (by default): extra small (xs), small (sm), medium (md), large (lg), and extra large (xl). These breakpoints allow developers to control the layout across different devices.

Flexbox

Bootstrap 5 heavily utilizes Flexbox, a CSS layout model that allows for efficient space distribution and alignment capabilities in a container. Flexbox makes it easier to design complex layouts without using floats and positioning.

Responsive Utilities

Bootstrap includes various responsive utility classes that show or hide elements based on screen size. For instance, .d-none and .d-md-block will hide an element on small screens and display it on medium-sized screens and above.

Media Queries

While Bootstrap handles most of the responsive design through its classes, understanding media queries is still important. Media queries allow for custom CSS based on the viewport size. For example:

```
@media (max-width: 768px) {

body {

background-color: lightblue;

}

}
```

This media query changes the body background color on screens smaller than 768 pixels.

Images and Responsiveness

Bootstrap 5 provides classes to make images responsive. By adding the .img-fluid class to an image, it ensures the image scales nicely to the parent element.

Typography and Responsiveness

Bootstrap 5 scales typography for different screen sizes. Using relative units like rem for font sizes, along with viewport-based sizing, helps in maintaining readability across devices.

Containers

Containers are used to pad and align content within a page. Bootstrap offers different container classes, like .container for a responsive fixed-width container and .container-fluid for a full-width container.

Viewport Meta Tag

The viewport meta tag is essential for responsive design. It should be included in the HTML to control the layout on mobile browsers:

```
<meta name="viewport" content="width=device-width, initial-scale=1">
```

Testing Responsiveness

Testing is a crucial part of responsive design. This involves checking the website on various devices and using browser tools to simulate different screen sizes.

Conclusion

The core concepts of responsive design in Bootstrap 5 are geared towards creating websites that work seamlessly across different devices and screen sizes. Understanding these concepts is essential for any web developer looking to build modern, responsive websites. Bootstrap's grid system, utility classes, and responsive components provide a robust foundation for this purpose.

1.5. Exploring the Bootstrap 5 Documentation

Bootstrap 5's documentation is a comprehensive guide that covers all aspects of the framework, from basic usage to advanced customization. It is an essential resource for developers working with Bootstrap, providing clear instructions, examples, and explanations of the framework's components and utilities.

Navigating the Documentation

The Bootstrap documentation is structured to be user-friendly and easy to navigate. The main sections are divided into various categories like 'Layout', 'Content', 'Forms', 'Components', and 'Helpers'. Each section provides detailed information about specific features and functionalities.

Getting Started Section

The 'Getting Started' section is the starting point for new users. It includes information on how to download Bootstrap, set up your project, and use the Bootstrap CDN. This section is crucial for understanding the basic setup required before delving into more advanced features.

Layout

The 'Layout' section explains Bootstrap's grid system, container classes, and utilities for spacing, display, and flexbox. It provides insights into creating responsive layouts and aligning content effectively.

Content

The 'Content' section covers typography, images, tables, and figures. It demonstrates how to use Bootstrap to style text, embed images, and format tables for a clean and responsive look.

Components

This is one of the most extensive sections in the documentation. It provides details on using various Bootstrap components like navbars, carousels, modals, and tooltips. Each component is accompanied by examples and code snippets, showing how to implement and customize them.

Forms

The 'Forms' section guides you through creating and styling forms using Bootstrap. It includes information on form layouts, input types, validation, and custom form elements.

Utilities

Utilities are a set of CSS classes for common styling tasks like margin and padding, text alignment, and color. The documentation thoroughly explains each utility class, helping to speed up the development process by reducing the need for custom CSS.

Helpers

Helpers are classes that provide solutions to common styling challenges. These include classes for clear fixes, positioning, and visibility. The documentation provides a complete list of these classes and their uses.

Customization

Bootstrap 5 offers extensive customization options. The documentation guides you through customizing components, changing colors, and adapting the framework to meet your specific design needs. This section is particularly useful for developers looking to create a unique look while leveraging Bootstrap's functionality.

Extending Bootstrap

For more advanced users, the documentation provides information on extending Bootstrap with custom JavaScript, using Bootstrap with various JavaScript frameworks, and contributing to the Bootstrap source code.

Accessibility

Bootstrap places a strong emphasis on accessibility. The documentation includes guidelines and best practices for creating accessible web content, ensuring that websites built with Bootstrap are usable by as many people as possible.

Version Migration

For those migrating from previous versions of Bootstrap, the documentation offers a detailed migration guide. This guide outlines the major changes and provides tips for a smooth transition.

Examples and Templates

The Bootstrap documentation includes a range of examples and templates to kickstart your projects. These practical resources demonstrate how to combine various Bootstrap components and utilities effectively.

Community and Support

The documentation also provides information on how to get help and contribute to the Bootstrap community. This includes links to the official Bootstrap blog, GitHub repository, and community forums.

Regular Updates

The Bootstrap team regularly updates the documentation to reflect new features, bug fixes, and improvements. It's advisable to check the documentation periodically for the latest information and best practices.

Conclusion

Exploring the Bootstrap 5 documentation is key to understanding and effectively utilizing the framework. Whether you're a beginner or an experienced developer, the documentation offers valuable resources, guidelines, and examples to enhance your web development projects with Bootstrap.

Chapter 2: Basic Components and Layout

2.1. Understanding Grid System

The grid system in Bootstrap is a fundamental concept that facilitates responsive and flexible web page layouts. It's a powerful tool for creating complex designs with ease and precision. Understanding how it works is crucial for any developer working with Bootstrap.

The Basics of Bootstrap Grid

Bootstrap's grid system uses a series of containers, rows, and columns to layout and align content. It's built with flexbox and allows up to 12 columns across the page. The grid system is responsive and columns will re-arrange depending on the screen size.

Containers

Containers are the most basic layout element in Bootstrap and are required when using the grid system. They are used to contain, pad, and align your content within a fixed or full-width setting. There are two container classes:

- .container, which sets a max-width at each responsive breakpoint
- .container-fluid, which is width: 100% at all breakpoints

Rows

A row in Bootstrap is used to group your columns horizontally. Each row is a flex container, allowing the columns within to automatically resize and align.

Columns

Columns are the immediate children of rows. You can use one of the twelve .col- classes to specify the number of columns you want to use out of the possible 12. For example, using .col-6 will make the column span half the width of the row.

Responsive Columns

Bootstrap's grid includes five tiers of predefined classes for building complex responsive layouts. These tiers are based on the width of the screen:

- Extra small (<576px)
- Small (≥576px)
- Medium (≥768px)
- Large (≥992px)
- Extra large (≥1200px)

Using Breakpoints

With the grid system, you can set different column sizes for different breakpoints. For example, .col-md-4 will set the column to 4/12 of the container for medium devices and larger.

Auto-Layout Columns

Bootstrap also offers auto-layout columns with .col. This feature automatically sizes columns based on the content within.

Column Wrapping

If more than 12 columns are placed within a single row, they will wrap onto a new line.

Column Ordering

You can change the visual order of columns using .order- classes. For example, .order-1 will place the column first, regardless of where it is in the HTML.

Nesting

To nest your content with the grid, add a new .row and set of .col- classes within an existing .col- class. This is useful for creating complex layouts.

Offsetting Columns

Offset classes can be used to increase the margin on the left side of a column. For instance, .offset-md-4 will push the column over four columns on medium and larger devices.

Alignment

You can align columns vertically and horizontally in a row using alignment classes such as .align-items-start, .justify-content-center, and more.

Example of a Simple Grid Layout

Here's a basic example of a Bootstrap grid layout:

```
<div class="container">

<div class="row">

<div class="col-md-8">.col-md-8</div>

<div class="col-md-4">.col-md-4</div>

</div>

</div>
```

Conclusion

The Bootstrap grid system is a robust and flexible tool that makes responsive layout design simpler and more efficient. By mastering the grid system, you can create various layouts that adapt to different screen sizes, enhancing the overall user experience of your web applications.

2.2. Utilizing Containers and Rows

In Bootstrap, containers and rows are fundamental building blocks for creating layouts. They work in conjunction with the grid system to structure and align content in a versatile and responsive manner. Understanding how to effectively use containers and rows is key to mastering layout design in Bootstrap.

Containers Overview

Containers are used to encapsulate and align your site's content. They can be fixed-width or full-width:

- .container: A responsive fixed-width container that changes size at different breakpoints.
- .container-fluid: A full-width container that spans the entire width of the viewport.

Implementing a Fixed-Width Container

A fixed-width container centers your content and aligns it with a consistent padding. It's responsive, meaning its width changes at different breakpoints. Here's an example:

```
<div class="container">

<!—Content here—>

</div>
```

Implementing a Full-Width Container

A full-width container extends the entire width of the viewport, making it useful for layouts that require edge-to-edge content. For example:

```
<div class="container-fluid">

<!—Content here—>

</div>
```

Understanding Rows in Bootstrap

Rows are crucial when using the Bootstrap grid system. They are used to create horizontal groups of columns and must be placed within a container.

Creating a Basic Row

Rows are wrappers for columns. Each row is a flex container which allows columns to flexibly resize and reposition. Here's a simple example:

```
<div class="container">

<div class="row">

<!—Columns here—>

</div>

</div>
```

The Role of Rows in the Grid System

In the grid system, rows are used to create horizontal groupings of columns. This ensures proper alignment and distribution of space among items in a row.

Handling Gutter Spacing

Gutters are the spacing between your columns. You can adjust gutter width with gutter classes (gx-* for horizontal gutters and gy-* for vertical gutters). For example:

```
<div class="row gx-5">

<!—Columns with horizontal spacing—>

</div>
```

No-Gutters Class

If you need to remove the space between columns, use the .no-gutters class on your row:

```
<div class="row no-gutters">

<!—Columns without spacing—>

</div>
```

Nested Rows

You can nest rows within columns to create more complex layouts. This is done by adding a new .row inside an existing column:

```
<div class="container">

<div class="row">

<div class="col-sm">

<div class="row">

<!—Nested columns here—>

</div>

</div>

</div>

</div>
```

Alignment and Justification

Bootstrap provides utility classes for aligning items within a row both vertically and horizontally, such as .align-items-center or .justify-content-between.

Responsive Behavior of Rows

Rows in Bootstrap are flex containers, meaning they are responsive by default. Columns within a row will stack vertically on smaller screens and lay out horizontally on larger screens.

Mixing Containers

You can mix different types of containers to create varied layouts. For example, using a .container-fluid for a full-width header and a .container for the main content area.

Practical Example of Containers and Rows

Here's a practical example combining containers and rows with columns:

```
<div class="container">

<div class="row">

<div class="col-md-8">.col-md-8</div>

<div class="col-md-4">.col-md-4</div>

</div>

</div>
```

Conclusion

Containers and rows are essential components of Bootstrap's grid system. They provide the structure and alignment necessary for creating responsive and flexible layouts. By understanding and utilizing these elements effectively, you can create diverse and responsive designs that cater to a wide range of devices and screen sizes.

2.3. Implementing Basic Components: Buttons, Forms, and Navbars

Bootstrap offers a wide range of components that are essential for building modern websites. Among these, buttons, forms, and navbars are some of the most frequently used elements. Understanding how to implement these components effectively is crucial for efficient web design.

Buttons in Bootstrap

Buttons are a fundamental part of any user interface, and Bootstrap provides a variety of styles and sizes to cater to different use cases.

Basic Button Syntax

To create a button in Bootstrap, use the <button> tag with the class .btn, followed by a style class like .btn-primary:

```
<button type="button" class="btn btn-primary">Primary Button</button>
```

Button Sizes

You can change the size of a button using .btn-lg for large buttons or .btn-sm for small buttons:

```
<button type="button" class="btn btn-primary btn-lg">Large Button</button>
```

Button States

Bootstrap also includes classes for different button states like disabled (disabled attribute) or active (.active class).

Forms in Bootstrap

Forms are key to gathering input from users, and Bootstrap simplifies the process of creating them.

Basic Form Structure

A basic Bootstrap form is structured with <form> elements, using form groups (.form-group) to wrap labels and form controls:

```
<form>

<div class="form-group">

<label for="inputEmail">Email address</label>

<input type="email" class="form-control" id="inputEmail" placeholder="Enter email">

</div>

</form>
```

Input Types

Bootstrap supports various input types like text, password, checkboxes, and radios, each styled for a consistent look and feel.

Validation States

Bootstrap provides styles for validation feedback with classes like .is-valid and .is-invalid to indicate the state of form controls.

Navbars in Bootstrap

Navbars are an essential component for any website's navigation, and Bootstrap offers a responsive and customizable navbar component.

Basic Navbar Structure

A basic Bootstrap navbar includes the <nav> element with a series of navigation links, forms, buttons, or text:

```
<nav class="navbar navbar-expand-lg navbar-light bg-light">

<!—Navbar content—>

</nav>
```

Responsive Behavior

Bootstrap's navbar is responsive by default. Using the .navbar-expand-* class, you can control at which breakpoint the navbar collapses into a hamburger menu.

Brand and Links

Adding a brand or navigation links to the navbar is straightforward:

```
<nav class="navbar navbar-light bg-light">

<a class="navbar-brand" href="#">Navbar</a>

<ul class="navbar-nav">

<li class="nav-item"><a class="nav-link" href="#">Home</a></li>

<!—More nav items—>

</ul>

</nav>
```

Dropdowns and Toggles

Navbars can also include dropdown menus and toggles for compact navigation in smaller viewports.

Integrating Components

These components can be integrated to create functional and aesthetically pleasing interfaces. For instance, a navbar can include form elements for a search bar, or buttons can be used within forms for submissions.

Customizing Components

Bootstrap components can be customized with additional CSS or by using the various available classes that Bootstrap provides. This allows for a high degree of personalization while maintaining consistency in design.

Practical Examples

In practice, these components are often used together to create a cohesive user interface. For example, a navbar at the top of a page for navigation, buttons for actions like submitting forms or changing settings, and forms for user input and interactions.

Conclusion

Implementing basic components like buttons, forms, and navbars is a foundational skill in Bootstrap. These components are versatile and can be customized to fit the needs of nearly any web project. Understanding how to use them effectively allows for the creation of intuitive and visually appealing user interfaces.

2.4. Styling Text and Images

Bootstrap provides a comprehensive set of utilities and classes for styling text and images, making it easy to create visually appealing and responsive web pages. Understanding how to effectively utilize these tools is essential for any web designer or developer working with Bootstrap.

Text Utilities

Bootstrap includes various utilities for styling text, such as alignment, wrapping, weight, and color.

Text Alignment

You can align text using classes like .text-center, .text-left, and .text-right. For example:

```
<p class="text-center">This text is centered.</p>
```

Text Wrapping and Overflow

Classes like .text-wrap and .text-nowrap control the wrapping of text. Overflow can be managed with .text-truncate to cut off text with an ellipsis.

Text Transformation

Transform the case of your text with .text-lowercase, .text-uppercase, and .text-capitalize.

Font Weight and Italics

Change font weight with .font-weight-bold or .font-weight-normal. Italics can be applied with .font-italic.

Color Utilities

Bootstrap provides a palette of contextual color classes for text, such as .text-primary, .text-success, and .text-danger.

Display Headings

For larger headings, Bootstrap offers .display-1 to .display-4 classes:

```
<h1 class="display-1">Display 1</h1>
```

Blockquotes

For quoting blocks of content from another source, use the <blockquote> element with Bootstrap classes for styling:

```
<blockquote class="blockquote">

<p class="mb-0">Lorem ipsum dolor sit amet...</p>
```

```
</blockquote>
```

Lists

Unstyled and inline lists can be created using .list-unstyled and .list-inline.

Responsive Images

Bootstrap's .img-fluid class ensures images are responsive and scales with the parent element.

```
<img src="image.jpg" class="img-fluid" alt="Responsive image">
```

Image Thumbnails

To create image thumbnails with a border, use the .img-thumbnail class:

```
<img src="image.jpg" class="img-thumbnail" alt="...">
```

Aligning Images

Align images using Bootstrap's float classes (.float-left or .float-right) or the newer flex classes.

Figures

Wrap images and captions in a <figure> with <figcaption> for semantic styling of images with captions:

```
<figure class="figure">

<img src="image.jpg" class="figure-img img-fluid rounded" alt="...">
```

<figcaption **class**="figure-caption">A caption for the above image.</**figcaption>**

</**figure>**

Text and Image Combinations

Combining text and images effectively can be achieved using Bootstrap's grid system or utility classes for alignment and spacing.

Customizing Styles

While Bootstrap provides a solid foundation, you can further customize the styles using custom CSS.

Accessibility

Ensure text and images are accessible, providing alternative text for images and sufficient contrast for text.

Conclusion

Bootstrap's text and image styling capabilities provide a quick and efficient way to create attractive, responsive, and accessible content. By mastering these utilities and classes, you can enhance the visual impact and usability of your web projects.

2.5. Responsive Utilities and Breakpoints

Bootstrap 5 offers an array of responsive utilities and breakpoints that are integral to designing a responsive and adaptive web layout. These utilities provide the flexibility to control the layout and appearance of elements based on the size of the user's screen.

Understanding Breakpoints

Breakpoints in Bootstrap are predefined points at which the website's layout will adjust to accommodate different screen sizes. The default breakpoints are:

- Extra small (xs): under 576px
- Small (sm): 576px and above
- Medium (md): 768px and above
- Large (lg): 992px and above
- Extra large (xl): 1200px and above
- Extra extra large (xxl): 1400px and above

Responsive Display Classes

Bootstrap's display utility classes (d-*) control the display of elements. You can show or hide elements at specific breakpoints using these classes. For example, .d-none .d-md-block will hide an element on small screens and display it on medium screens and larger.

Flexbox Utilities

Flexbox utilities in Bootstrap make it easy to design complex layouts. Classes like .d-flex, .flex-row, and .flex-column help in aligning and distributing items within a container.

Spacing Utilities

Bootstrap provides spacing utilities for margin (m-*) and padding (p-*). These classes include responsive variants to adjust spacing at different breakpoints. For instance, mt-3 mt-md-5 applies a margin-top of 3 on all sizes and 5 on medium and larger screens.

Text Alignment

Text alignment can be controlled with classes like .text-center, .text-md-left, etc., allowing you to align text differently at various breakpoints.

Responsive Font Sizes

Bootstrap's responsive font sizes automatically adjust text sizing based on the viewport size, enhancing readability across devices.

Visibility Classes

Visibility classes like .visible or .invisible, along with their responsive variations, control the visibility of elements without affecting the layout.

Ordering and Positioning

With flexbox utilities, you can reorder elements using .order- classes and control their alignment with .align-self-, .justify-content-, and .align-items- classes.

Grid Breakpoints

The grid system in Bootstrap also responds to breakpoints. Column classes like .col-md-6 mean the element will use half the container width on medium devices and above.

Using Breakpoints with Grid Columns

You can mix and match different column sizes for different breakpoints. For example, .col-12 .col-md-6 makes an element full width on small screens and half-width on medium and larger screens.

Responsive Image Classes

Images can be made responsive with .img-fluid, ensuring they scale with the parent element.

Customizing Breakpoints

For advanced use-cases, you can customize Bootstrap's breakpoints via SASS variables, tailoring the responsive behavior to your specific needs.

Responsive Embeds

For responsive embedded content like videos, use the .embed-responsive class along with an aspect ratio class (e.g., .embed-responsive-16by9).

Utility APIs

Bootstrap 5 introduces a utility API for creating custom utility classes, giving you even more control over responsive design.

Conclusion

Bootstrap's responsive utilities and breakpoints are essential tools for creating modern, responsive web designs. They provide the flexibility to create layouts that look great on any device, ensuring a consistent and user-friendly experience. Understanding and effectively utilizing these tools is key to successful responsive web development.

Chapter 3: Advanced Components

3.1. Cards and Accordions: Designing Complex Layouts

Bootstrap's card and accordion components are versatile tools for creating more complex and visually appealing layouts. They can be used for a wide range of content, including text, images, links, and more, making them essential for modern web design.

Understanding Cards in Bootstrap

Cards are flexible content containers with multiple variants and options. They can hold a wide variety of content, including text, images, lists, and more.

Basic Card Structure

A basic card in Bootstrap is created with the .card class. This can include header, body, and footer sections:

```
<div class="card">

<div class="card-header">Header</div>

<div class="card-body">

<h5 class="card-title">Card title</h5>

<p class="card-text">Some quick example text...</p>

</div>

<div class="card-footer">Footer</div>
```

```
</div>
```

Card Images

You can add images to cards by using the .card-img-top or .card-img-bottom class:

```
<div class="card">

<img src="image.jpg" class="card-img-top" alt="...">

<div class="card-body">

<p class="card-text">Card content here.</p>

</div>

</div>
```

Card Layouts

Cards can be organized in various layouts, such as grid columns or horizontal layouts, for more complex designs.

Grid Columns

Using the Bootstrap grid system, you can place multiple cards in a row:

```
<div class="row">

<div class="col-sm-4">

<div class="card">

<!—Card content—>
```

```
</div>

</div>

<!—More cards—>

</div>
```

Horizontal Layout

For a horizontal card layout, use the .card-horizontal class along with the grid system.

Card Styles

Bootstrap offers various styles to customize the appearance of cards, such as background colors, border colors, and more.

Understanding Accordions

Accordions are a great way to display content in a collapsible format, ideal for FAQs, informational panels, and more.

Basic Accordion Structure

An accordion in Bootstrap is created using the .accordion class along with card components:

```
<div class="accordion" id="accordionExample">

<div class="card">

<div class="card-header" id="headingOne">

<!—Header content—>
```

```
</div>

<div id="collapseOne" class="collapse show"
aria-labelledby="headingOne"
data-parent="#accordionExample">

<div class="card-body">

<!—Collapsible content—>

</div>

</div>

</div>

<!—More accordion items—>

</div>
```

Customizing Accordions

Accordions can be customized with different styles, colors, and behaviors to fit the design of your site.

Combining Cards and Accordions

Cards and accordions can be combined to create complex, interactive layouts. For example, using cards as accordion headers or embedding accordions within cards.

Responsive Behavior

Both cards and accordions are responsive by default, making them suitable for various devices and screen sizes.

Advanced Card Techniques

You can further enhance cards with advanced techniques like card decks, card groups, and using utility classes for spacing and alignment.

Accessibility in Accordions

Ensure that accordions are accessible by providing appropriate ARIA attributes and keyboard navigation.

Conclusion

Cards and accordions in Bootstrap provide a sophisticated way to present content in a structured, visually appealing manner. They are highly customizable and responsive, making them ideal for a wide range of web design applications. By mastering these components, you can enhance the user experience and aesthetic appeal of your websites.

3.2. Carousel: Creating Interactive Slideshows

Bootstrap's Carousel component is a versatile tool for creating interactive slideshows, perfect for showcasing images, content, or other elements in a rotating slider format. This feature enhances user engagement and adds dynamic visual elements to a website.

Basic Carousel Structure

A Bootstrap carousel is structured using a combination of HTML, CSS, and JavaScript. The basic setup includes a wrapper element with the .carousel class, a .carousel-inner container for slides, and individual .carousel-item elements for each slide:

```
<div id="carouselExampleIndicators" class="carousel slide" data-ride="carousel">

<div class="carousel-inner">

<div class="carousel-item active">

<img src="image1.jpg" class="d-block w-100" alt="...">

</div>

<div class="carousel-item">

<img src="image2.jpg" class="d-block w-100" alt="...">

</div>

<!—More carousel items—>

</div>

</div>
```

Adding Carousel Controls

To navigate between slides, Bootstrap provides previous and next controls. These are HTML anchor tags with specific classes and data attributes:

```
<a class="carousel-control-prev" href="#carouselExampleIndicators" role="button" data-slide="prev">

<span class="carousel-control-prev-icon" aria-hidden="true"></span>

<span class="sr-only">Previous</span>
```

```
</a>

<a class="carousel-control-next"
href="#carouselExampleIndicators" role="button"
data-slide="next">

<span class="carousel-control-next-icon"
aria-hidden="true"></span>

<span class="sr-only">Next</span>

</a>
```

Indicators for the Carousel

Carousel indicators allow users to jump to a specific slide. They are typically represented as a series of dots or lines at the bottom of the carousel:

```
<ol class="carousel-indicators">

<li data-target="#carouselExampleIndicators" data-slide-to="0"
class="active"></li>

<li data-target="#carouselExampleIndicators"
data-slide-to="1"></li>

<!—More indicators—>

</ol>
```

Adding Captions

To provide context or additional information, you can include captions using the .carousel-caption class within each .carousel-item:

```
<div class="carousel-item">
```

```
<img src="image.jpg" class="d-block w-100" alt="...">

<div class="carousel-caption d-none d-md-block">

<h5>Slide Title</h5>

<p>Slide Description</p>

</div>

</div>
```

Animating Slides

Bootstrap's Carousel component includes built-in animations for transitioning between slides. These can be customized with additional CSS or overridden for different effects.

Auto-Play and Interval

By default, the carousel automatically cycles through slides. You can control this behavior and set the interval between slides using data attributes.

Pausing the Carousel

The carousel can be paused on hover or on focus, which is useful for allowing users to interact with the content on each slide.

Implementing Fade Effect

Apart from the default sliding effect, Bootstrap also provides a fade effect for transitioning between slides. This is achieved by adding the .carousel-fade class to your carousel.

Responsive Images

Ensure your carousel images are responsive by using the .img-fluid class and appropriately sizing your images for different screen resolutions.

Advanced Customization

For more advanced customization, you can use Bootstrap's utility classes or write custom CSS and JavaScript to modify the appearance and behavior of the carousel.

Accessibility Considerations

Make sure your carousel is accessible by providing alternative text for images, using proper ARIA attributes, and ensuring keyboard navigability.

Conclusion

The Bootstrap Carousel component is a powerful tool for adding interactive and visually appealing slideshows to your website. By understanding and utilizing its various features and customization options, you can create engaging experiences that captivate your audience.

3.3. Modal Dialogs and Popovers

Modal dialogs and popovers are two of the interactive components provided by Bootstrap that add a layer of engagement to websites. They are useful for displaying additional information, gathering user input, and guiding user interactions without leaving the current page.

Understanding Modals in Bootstrap

A modal is a dialog box/popup window that is displayed on top of the current page. It is typically used for user notifications, form submissions, or to display additional content.

Basic Modal Structure

Creating a basic modal involves defining the HTML structure with a series of div elements and Bootstrap classes:

```
<div class="modal fade" id="exampleModal" tabindex="-1" aria-labelledby="exampleModalLabel" aria-hidden="true">

<div class="modal-dialog">

<div class="modal-content">

<div class="modal-header">

<h5 class="modal-title" id="exampleModalLabel">Modal Title</h5>

<button type="button" class="close" data-dismiss="modal" aria-label="Close">

<span aria-hidden="true">&times;</span>

</button>

</div>

<div class="modal-body">

<!—Modal content here—>

</div>
```

```
<div class="modal-footer">

<button type="button" class="btn btn-secondary" data-dismiss="modal">Close</button>

<button type="button" class="btn btn-primary">Save changes</button>

</div>

</div>

</div>

</div>
```

Triggering Modals

Modals are typically triggered by a button or link. You can use the data-toggle="modal" and data-target="#exampleModal" attributes to link a trigger element to a modal:

```
<button type="button" class="btn btn-primary" data-toggle="modal" data-target="#exampleModal">

Launch demo modal

</button>
```

Customizing Modals

You can customize modals in various ways, such as changing sizes (using .modal-lg or .modal-sm), modifying the header, body, and footer content, or adding animations.

Using Popovers

Popovers are small overlays of content, similar to tooltips but capable of displaying more content. They are perfect for adding explanations or additional information to elements.

Creating a Popover

A popover is attached to an element and activated by a click or hover. Here's an example of attaching a popover to a button:

<button **type**="button" **class**="btn btn-secondary" **data-toggle**="popover" **title**="Popover title" **data-content**="Some popover content">

Click to toggle popover

</button>

Customizing Popovers

Bootstrap allows the customization of popovers, including changing their titles, content, and placement (top, bottom, left, right).

Controlling Popover Behavior

You can control the behavior of popovers, such as how they are triggered (click, hover, focus), and whether they should be dismissed automatically.

Modals and Forms

Modals can be combined with forms to create interactive dialogs for user inputs, such as login forms, registration forms, or data entry forms.

Animating Modals and Popovers

Both modals and popovers support transition animations, which can be customized or replaced with custom animations.

Accessibility in Modals and Popovers

Ensuring accessibility in modals and popovers is crucial. This includes managing focus, using ARIA attributes, and ensuring keyboard navigation.

Responsive Considerations

Modals and popovers should be tested for responsiveness, ensuring they appear and function correctly across different devices and screen sizes.

Advanced Interactions

For advanced use cases, you can add JavaScript to enhance the functionality of modals and popovers, like loading content dynamically or handling form submissions.

Conclusion

Modals and popovers are powerful components in Bootstrap's toolkit, offering a range of possibilities for enhancing user interaction on websites. Understanding their structure, customization options, and best practices for use and accessibility ensures that they can be effectively integrated into modern web projects.

3.4. Customizing Bootstrap Tables

Bootstrap tables provide a clean and responsive way to display data. Customizing these tables allows you to enhance their functionality and appearance to suit the specific needs of your website or application.

Basic Table Structure

A basic Bootstrap table is created with the <table> tag combined with the .table class:

```
<table class="table">

<!—Table rows and columns—>

</table>
```

Responsive Tables

To make a table responsive, wrap it within a .table-responsive div. This makes the table horizontally scrollable on small devices:

```
<div class="table-responsive">

<table class="table">

<!—Table rows and columns—>

</table>

</div>
```

Striped Rows

For better readability, you can add zebra-striping to any table row within the <tbody> using the .table-striped class:

```
<table class="table table-striped">
<!—Table rows and columns—>
</table>
```

Bordered Tables

Add borders on all sides of the table and cells with the .table-bordered class:

```
<table class="table table-bordered">
<!—Table rows and columns—>
</table>
```

Hoverable Rows

To enable a hover state on table rows, use the .table-hover class:

```
<table class="table table-hover">
<!—Table rows and columns—>
</table>
```

Small Tables

For making tables more compact by cutting cell padding in half, use the .table-sm class:

```
<table class="table table-sm">
<!—Table rows and columns—>
</table>
```

Dark Table

You can also opt for a dark-themed table using the .table-dark class, which changes the color of text and backgrounds:

```
<table class="table table-dark">

<!—Table rows and columns—>

</table>
```

Colored Tables

Bootstrap provides contextual classes to color tables based on various states like success, warning, or danger:

```
<table class="table table-success">

<!—Table rows and columns—>

</table>
```

Table Head Options

Customize the <thead> with light or dark themes using .thead-light or .thead-dark:

```
<thead class="thead-light">

<!—Table header rows and columns—>

</thead>
```

Breakpoint Specific Responsive Tables

For more control over the responsiveness, you can use classes like .table-responsive-md to make the table scrollable only on certain breakpoints.

Custom Content

Inside table cells, you can add any type of content like buttons, badges, or forms, and style them as needed.

Interactive Elements

Adding interactive elements like dropdowns or modals within table cells can enhance functionality.

Custom Styling

Although Bootstrap provides a range of styling options, you can further customize tables with your own CSS to meet specific design requirements.

JavaScript Enhancements

Enhance tables with JavaScript for features like sorting, filtering, or dynamically loading data.

Accessibility Considerations

Ensure that your tables are accessible by using correct semantic markup and attributes like scope for table headers.

Conclusion

Customizing Bootstrap tables allows you to adapt their functionality and appearance to better fit the data display requirements of your website or application. With Bootstrap's built-in classes and the ability to add your own styles and functionality, you can create tables that are both attractive and user-friendly.

3.5. Tabs and Pills for Content Organization

Tabs and pills in Bootstrap are powerful components for organizing content in a compact and interactive manner. They allow for the effective display of different content types within the same space, enhancing user engagement and experience.

Understanding Tabs in Bootstrap

Tabs in Bootstrap are used to toggle between different views or content sections within the same container.

Basic Tab Structure

A basic tab setup involves a list of links or buttons used as the tab controls, and corresponding content panes. Here's an example structure:

```
<ul class="nav nav-tabs" id="myTab" role="tablist">

<li class="nav-item">

<a class="nav-link active" id="home-tab" data-toggle="tab" href="#home" role="tab" aria-controls="home" aria-selected="true">Home</a>

</li>

<!—More tab items—>

</ul>

<div class="tab-content" id="myTabContent">

<div class="tab-pane fade show active" id="home" role="tabpanel" aria-labelledby="home-tab">
```

<!—Tab content—>

</div>

<!—More content panes—>

</div>

Creating Pills

Pills are similar to tabs but are styled differently, appearing as rounded buttons. They are created using the .nav-pills class instead of .nav-tabs.

Controlling Active States

Bootstrap automatically manages the active states of tabs and pills based on user interaction, but you can also control this manually through JavaScript or by applying the .active class.

Vertical Tabs and Pills

You can create vertical tabs or pills by stacking the .nav items and using grid layout or utility classes for alignment.

Using Dropdowns in Tabs

Tabs and pills can include dropdown menus for organizing additional content under a single tab item.

Dynamic Tab Content

You can dynamically load content into tabs using JavaScript, which is particularly useful for loading content via AJAX.

Fade Effect on Tab Change

For a smoother transition between tab content, you can use the .fade class to add a fading effect.

Customizing Tabs and Pills

Customize the appearance of tabs and pills with additional CSS for things like colors, borders, and hover effects.

Nested Tabs

Tabs and pills can be nested within one another to create more complex content structures.

Accessibility in Tabs

Ensure accessibility by using appropriate ARIA attributes and roles, particularly for users who rely on screen readers and keyboard navigation.

Responsive Behavior

Tabs and pills are responsive, but for complex layouts, consider how they will reflow on smaller screens. Collapsible or dropdown formats might be more suitable for mobile devices.

Tabs with Card Integration

Tabs can be integrated with Bootstrap cards, placing the tab navigation within the card header and the content within the card body.

Handling Events

Bootstrap's JavaScript API allows you to handle events on tab show, hide, or when the state changes, giving you greater control over the behavior.

Conclusion

Tabs and pills are versatile components for organizing content in a user-friendly way. They allow for a neat and effective presentation of various content types, making them ideal for use in settings such as dashboards, product pages, or informational sections. By mastering these components, you can enhance the structure and interactivity of your web projects.

Chapter 4: Customization and Theming

4.1. Overriding Default Styles with CSS

Customizing Bootstrap to fit the unique style and branding of your website is essential for creating a distinctive online presence. Overriding Bootstrap's default styles with your own CSS is a straightforward process that allows for extensive customization.

Understanding Bootstrap's CSS

Bootstrap's default styles are defined using CSS classes. To customize these styles, you need to understand how they are structured and how to effectively override them.

The Importance of Specificity

CSS specificity determines which styles are applied when there are multiple conflicting rules. Increasing the specificity of your custom styles ensures they override Bootstrap's defaults.

Using Custom Stylesheets

Create a custom stylesheet and link it after the Bootstrap CSS file in your HTML. This ensures that your styles take precedence:

```
<link href="bootstrap.css" rel="stylesheet">

<link href="custom.css" rel="stylesheet">
```

Overriding Styles

To override a Bootstrap style, use the same selector used by Bootstrap and then specify your custom styles:

```
.btn-primary {

background-color: #yourColor;

}
```

Customizing Components

Target specific Bootstrap components in your CSS to alter their appearance. For example, to change the look of all buttons:

```
.btn {

border-radius: 0;

}
```

Utilizing CSS Preprocessors

If you're using a CSS preprocessor like SASS or LESS, you can customize Bootstrap's source CSS more effectively by modifying variables and mixins.

Responsive Customizations

Consider responsive design when customizing styles. Use media queries to apply different styles based on the viewport size:

```
@media (min-width: 768px) {

.navbar {

background-color: #333;

}

}
```

Typography and Color Scheme

Customize the typography and color scheme to match your brand. Bootstrap's utility classes for text and background colors can be overridden to reflect your design:

```
.bg-primary {

background-color: #yourBrandColor !important;

}
```

Customizing the Grid System

If necessary, you can customize Bootstrap's grid system by altering the grid classes in your CSS or preprocessor files.

Hover and Focus States

Don't forget to customize the hover and focus states for interactive elements to maintain a cohesive design:

```
.btn-primary:hover {

background-color: #darkerYourColor;

}
```

Using !important Sparingly

Use !important judiciously to override Bootstrap styles, but be cautious as it can make future maintenance difficult.

Extending Bootstrap with New Classes

Instead of overriding existing classes, consider extending Bootstrap by creating new classes that apply your custom styles:

```
.btn-custom {
background-color: #uniqueColor;
}
```

Keeping Bootstrap Updatable

Organize your customizations in a way that doesn't hinder updating Bootstrap to a newer version. Avoid modifying the original Bootstrap files directly.

Testing Your Customizations

Thoroughly test your customizations across different browsers and devices to ensure consistent behavior and appearance.

Conclusion

Customizing Bootstrap's default styles allows you to tailor the framework to your specific design needs. By understanding how to effectively override and extend Bootstrap's CSS, you can create a unique and cohesive look for your website or application while retaining the benefits of the Bootstrap framework.

4.2. Creating Custom Themes with SASS

Bootstrap's use of SASS (Syntactically Awesome Stylesheets) is a powerful feature that allows for the creation of custom themes. SASS extends CSS with features like variables, nested rules, and mixins, making it easier to create and maintain complex stylesheets.

Understanding SASS in Bootstrap

Bootstrap's source code is written in SASS, which means you can use its variables, mixins, and functions to customize your theme.

Setting Up SASS

To start, you need to set up SASS in your development environment. This typically involves installing Node.js, which comes with npm (Node Package Manager), and then installing SASS through npm:

npm install -g sass

Customizing Variables

Bootstrap provides a set of SASS variables that you can override to change the look and feel of components. For instance, you can modify color, padding, border-radius, etc.:

$primary: #007bff;

$danger: #dc3545;

Using Mixins

Mixins are a powerful feature of SASS that let you create reusable styles. Bootstrap comes with a range of mixins that you can use or override in your custom themes.

Compiling SASS

After making your customizations, compile your SASS code into CSS. This can be done via the command line or using task runners like Gulp or Webpack.

Organizing Your Files

Keep your SASS files organized. Have a main file that imports Bootstrap's SASS files and your custom variables and styles.

Responsive Utilities

Leverage Bootstrap's responsive utilities in your SASS files to ensure that your theme is mobile-friendly.

Theming Components

You can create themes for individual components. For example, you can write SASS styles specifically for buttons, navbars, or modals.

Creating Dark Mode

With SASS, implementing a dark mode for your website becomes easier. You can define color variables for both light and dark modes and switch between them based on user preference.

Custom Functions

SASS allows you to write custom functions for complex style calculations or manipulations, further extending the customization capability.

Nested SASS

Take advantage of SASS's nesting feature to write concise and readable styles that closely match your HTML structure.

Using SASS Loops

SASS loops can be used to generate multiple styles dynamically, which is particularly useful for creating themes with multiple color schemes.

Best Practices

Follow best practices like using meaningful variable names, commenting your code, and keeping styles modular.

Updating Bootstrap

Be cautious when updating Bootstrap. Keep your custom SASS files separate to avoid conflicts when updating the Bootstrap source.

Performance Considerations

Optimize your final CSS for performance. Minify and concatenate files where possible to reduce load times.

Testing and Debugging

Test your custom styles across different browsers and devices to ensure consistency. SASS source maps can be helpful for debugging.

Conclusion

Creating custom themes with SASS in Bootstrap allows for extensive customization and fine control over the styling of your website. By leveraging SASS features in conjunction with Bootstrap's robust framework, you can design unique and responsive themes that stand out.

4.3. Utilizing Bootstrap Icons

Bootstrap Icons are a library of free, open-source icons designed to work seamlessly with Bootstrap components and utilities. Incorporating these icons into your projects enhances user interfaces with scalable, SVG-based symbols.

Introduction to Bootstrap Icons

Bootstrap Icons provide a wide range of glyphs for common UI actions and items. These icons are designed to be stylistically consistent with the Bootstrap framework.

Adding Bootstrap Icons

To use Bootstrap Icons, include the Bootstrap Icons stylesheet in your HTML. This can be done by linking to the CDN:

```
<link rel="stylesheet" href="https://cdn.jsdelivr.net/npm/bootstrap-icons@1.0.0/font/bootstrap-icons.css">
```

Alternatively, you can install the icon library via npm:

```
npm install bootstrap-icons
```

Using Icons in HTML

Once included, icons can be added to your HTML by using the <i> tag with the relevant class name. For example:

```
<i class="bi bi-alarm"></i>
```

Icon Sizing

Icons are scalable and can be sized using the font-size CSS property, or by using Bootstrap's size utility classes:

```
<i class="bi bi-alarm" style="font-size: 2rem;"></i>
```

Coloring Icons

Change the color of icons by applying CSS color styles:

```
<i class="bi bi-alarm" style="color: red;"></i>
```

Icons in Buttons and Links

Icons can be combined with Bootstrap's buttons and links to create visually appealing interactive elements:

```
<button class="btn btn-primary">

<i class="bi bi-star-fill"></i> Star

</button>
```

Icons in Forms

Enhance form inputs by adding icons for visual cues. This can be done by placing icon tags within form groups.

Accessibility with Icons

When using icons, particularly for interactive elements, ensure they are accessible. This includes using proper alt text or ARIA labels.

Customizing Icons with CSS

Further customize Bootstrap Icons using CSS for effects like hover transitions or rotation.

Using Icons in Navigation

Icons can be integrated into navigation elements like tabs, pills, or navbars to make them more intuitive.

Icons in Lists

Use icons in lists to replace traditional bullets or to signify list item types.

Loading Icons via JavaScript

Bootstrap Icons can also be loaded and manipulated via JavaScript for dynamic UI changes.

Creating Custom Icon Sets

If the existing Bootstrap Icons don't meet your needs, you can create custom icon sets by following the styling guidelines of Bootstrap Icons.

Performance Considerations

Consider the performance implications of using many icons, particularly when loading them from a CDN.

Conclusion

Bootstrap Icons are a valuable resource for enhancing the visual appeal and usability of your Bootstrap-based projects. Their integration into various components and utilities allows for the creation of more engaging and intuitive user interfaces.

4.4. Adaptive Color Schemes

Adaptive color schemes in web design are crucial for creating interfaces that are both aesthetically pleasing and user-friendly. Bootstrap provides tools and techniques for implementing color schemes that adapt to various user preferences and contexts.

Understanding Color Schemes in Bootstrap

Bootstrap comes with a predefined set of color schemes used throughout the framework. These include colors for text, background, buttons, and other components.

Utilizing Bootstrap Variables

Bootstrap's color schemes can be customized through SASS variables. You can override these variables to change the default color palette:

$primary: #5562eb;

$success: #28a745;

$info: #17a2b8;

Implementing Dark Mode

Dark mode is increasingly popular for its visual appeal and reduced eye strain in low-light conditions. You can implement a dark mode by adjusting the color variables and using media queries or JavaScript to toggle between light and dark themes.

Responsive Color Schemes

Ensure that your color schemes are responsive and provide a consistent experience across various devices and screen sizes.

Color Contrast for Accessibility

Maintain sufficient color contrast ratios to ensure accessibility for users with visual impairments. Bootstrap's color utility classes can be customized to improve contrast.

Customizing Component Colors

Beyond global color variables, you can also customize colors for specific components like buttons, navbars, or cards:

```
.btn-custom {

background-color: #yourColor;

&:hover {

background-color: darken(#yourColor, 10%);

}

}
```

Using Color Utilities

Bootstrap provides utility classes for text and background colors. These can be extended or overridden to fit your color scheme.

Creating Color Themes

Develop a set of color themes for your application that users can choose from. This could include high-contrast themes, colorblind-friendly palettes, or brand-specific themes.

CSS Custom Properties

Leverage CSS custom properties (CSS variables) for easier theming and real-time theme switching.

Theme Switcher

Implement a theme switcher in your UI, allowing users to select their preferred color scheme. This can be done using JavaScript to toggle between different stylesheets or modify CSS variables.

Dynamic Theming with JavaScript

Use JavaScript to dynamically change the color scheme based on user actions, time of day, or other external factors.

Testing Color Schemes

Test your color schemes across various devices and under different lighting conditions to ensure readability and visual comfort.

Integrating with User System Preferences

Detect and integrate with users' system preferences, such as dark mode settings, using media queries like prefers-color-scheme.

Documentation and Style Guide

Document your color schemes and guidelines in a style guide to maintain consistency across your project.

Performance Considerations

Be mindful of the performance impact of complex theming systems, especially when loading multiple stylesheets or using JavaScript for dynamic theming.

Conclusion

Adaptive color schemes are an essential aspect of modern web design, and Bootstrap provides a solid foundation for implementing them. By customizing Bootstrap's color variables, using utility classes, and considering user preferences and accessibility, you can create a visually appealing and user-friendly interface.

4.5. Design Consistency and Branding

Maintaining design consistency and aligning with branding guidelines is crucial for creating a cohesive and professional web presence. Bootstrap's flexibility and customization options make it an ideal framework for enforcing design standards and brand identity.

Importance of Design Consistency

Consistent design enhances user experience, builds brand recognition, and ensures that all elements of a website work harmoniously. Bootstrap's consistent and reusable components aid in achieving this.

Defining Brand Guidelines

Establish clear brand guidelines that include colors, fonts, logo usage, and tone of voice. These guidelines should inform all design decisions and be reflected in your Bootstrap customizations.

Customizing Bootstrap for Branding

Use Bootstrap's customization capabilities to tailor the framework to your brand. This includes modifying colors, typography, and component styles to match your brand identity.

Typography and Branding

Typography plays a significant role in branding. Customize Bootstrap's typography settings to align with your brand's fonts and typographic style.

$font-family-base: 'Your Brand Font', sans-serif;

Consistent Color Palette

Create a consistent color palette by customizing Bootstrap's color variables. Ensure that these colors are used consistently across all web pages and components.

Branding Components

Customize Bootstrap components to reflect your brand identity. This can include adding branded elements to navbars, footers, buttons, and more.

Reusable Components

Develop a library of reusable components that adhere to your branding guidelines. This ensures consistency across different parts of your website or application.

Responsive Design and Branding

Ensure that your branding is consistently applied across all device sizes. Bootstrap's responsive utilities can help achieve a uniform look on desktops, tablets, and mobile devices.

Consistency in Spacing and Layout

Maintain consistent spacing and layout throughout your website. Bootstrap's grid system and spacing utilities can be customized to adhere to your design standards.

Branding with Icons and Images

Incorporate your brand's icons and images into Bootstrap components. Ensure that these visual elements are used consistently and appropriately.

Overriding Bootstrap Defaults

Override Bootstrap's default styles carefully to maintain the framework's integrity while infusing your brand's identity.

Creating a Style Guide

Document your branding and design decisions in a style guide. This guide should be easily accessible to anyone working on your website.

Testing for Consistency

Regularly review your website to ensure that new additions or changes adhere to your established branding and design guidelines.

Training Your Team

Educate your team about your brand guidelines and the importance of maintaining design consistency. Encourage them to use the predefined styles and components.

Gathering Feedback

Periodically gather feedback on the effectiveness of your branding and design consistency. Be open to making adjustments based on user experience and feedback.

Updating Brand Elements

Keep your branding elements up-to-date and ensure that changes are reflected promptly across your website.

Conclusion

Bootstrap's customization capabilities make it an effective tool for maintaining design consistency and reinforcing brand identity. By carefully defining brand guidelines and applying them consistently throughout your Bootstrap-based project, you can create a cohesive and recognizable online presence.

Chapter 5: Working with Forms

5.1. Designing Effective Web Forms

Designing effective web forms is crucial in ensuring user engagement and enhancing the user experience. Bootstrap provides a comprehensive set of tools to create forms that are not only functional but also aesthetically pleasing and user-friendly.

Understanding the Importance of Form Design

Effective form design plays a key role in user interactions, from registration and login to feedback and purchases. The goal is to make forms intuitive, easy to use, and error-free.

Basic Form Structure in Bootstrap

Bootstrap forms start with a <form> element, utilizing various classes for different types of inputs, labels, and structure:

```
<form>

<div class="form-group">

<label for="inputEmail">Email address</label>

<input type="email" class="form-control" id="inputEmail" placeholder="Enter email">

</div>

<!—Additional form elements—>

</form>
```

Utilizing Grid Layout in Forms

Bootstrap's grid system can be used to create complex form layouts with multiple columns, ensuring forms are responsive and well-organized:

```
<div class="form-row">

<div class="col">

<input type="text" class="form-control" placeholder="First name">

</div>

<div class="col">

<input type="text" class="form-control" placeholder="Last name">

</div>

</div>
```

Designing Inline Forms

For a more compact form, Bootstrap provides the .form-inline class, allowing form elements to be displayed inline, primarily used for simple forms like search bars.

Using Form Controls

Bootstrap offers a variety of form controls, such as input, textarea, select, and range. These controls can be styled and customized to fit the design of the form.

Implementing Custom Checkboxes and Radios

Customize the appearance of checkboxes and radio buttons using Bootstrap's custom forms classes, enhancing the visual appeal and user experience:

```
<div class="custom-control custom-checkbox">

<input type="checkbox" class="custom-control-input" id="customCheck1">

<label class="custom-control-label" for="customCheck1">Check this custom checkbox</label>

</div>
```

Integrating Input Groups

Input groups allow the addition of text, buttons, or dropdown menus to form inputs. They are useful for search bars, login forms, and other interactive form fields.

Form Validation Styles

Bootstrap provides styles for valid and invalid form inputs, which can be used to give immediate feedback to users:

```
<div class="form-group">

<input type="text" class="form-control is-invalid">

<div class="invalid-feedback">

Please provide a valid city.

</div>

</div>
```

Focus on Accessibility

Ensure that forms are accessible by providing proper labels, using fieldsets for grouping related controls, and incorporating ARIA attributes where necessary.

Responsive and Mobile-Friendly Forms

Design forms with responsiveness in mind. Ensure that they are easy to navigate and fill out on all devices, especially on mobile.

Enhancing Forms with JavaScript

For more advanced form functionalities, like dynamic form fields or validation, use JavaScript in conjunction with Bootstrap's form components.

Form Customization

While Bootstrap provides a solid foundation, you can further customize forms with your CSS to better align with your website's design aesthetics.

Testing Form Design

Regularly test your forms for usability, ensuring they are intuitive and efficient. This can include user testing and feedback sessions.

Conclusion

Effective form design is essential in guiding users through an interaction with your website. Bootstrap's form components and utilities provide a solid foundation for creating forms that are not only functional but also visually appealing and user-friendly. By understanding and utilizing these tools, you can significantly enhance the user experience on your website.

5.2. Form Validation Techniques

Effective form validation is crucial in ensuring data integrity and improving user experience. Bootstrap provides built-in validation styles and tools that can be leveraged to create effective and user-friendly form validations.

Importance of Form Validation

Form validation helps in preventing incorrect data submission and provides users with necessary guidance to fill out forms correctly.

Client-Side Validation with Bootstrap

Bootstrap includes styles for client-side validation, allowing you to visually indicate the validity of form fields:

```
<div class="form-group">

<label for="inputEmail">Email address</label>

<input type="email" class="form-control is-invalid" id="inputEmail" placeholder="Enter email">

<div class="invalid-feedback">

Please enter a valid email address.

</div>

</div>
```

Using HTML5 Validation

Leverage HTML5 form attributes like required, type="email", and pattern for simple yet powerful client-side validation.

Custom Validation Messages

Customize validation messages to guide users effectively. Bootstrap's invalid feedback class can be used to display these messages:

<div class="invalid-feedback">

Your password must be at least 8 characters long.

</div>

Server-Side Validation

In addition to client-side validation, ensure that data is also validated on the server side for enhanced security and data integrity.

Real-Time Validation

Improve user experience by implementing real-time validation using JavaScript or jQuery to validate fields as the user types.

Styling Valid and Invalid Fields

Use Bootstrap's .is-valid and .is-invalid classes to style valid and invalid fields, providing immediate feedback to the user.

Accessibility in Form Validation

Make sure your validation is accessible by providing appropriate aria attributes and ensuring screen readers can read validation messages.

Grouping Form Controls for Validation

Group related form controls and validate them as a unit for better user experience, especially in complex forms.

Using Regular Expressions for Complex Patterns

For complex validation rules, use regular expressions in your JavaScript validation logic.

Dynamic Form Validation

For more complex scenarios, like forms that change based on user input, implement dynamic validation that adjusts according to the context.

Debouncing Validation Requests

Implement debouncing in JavaScript to delay validation until the user has stopped typing, reducing unnecessary processing and improving performance.

Tooltip and Popover for Validation Messages

Use Bootstrap's tooltips and popovers to display validation messages in a more interactive and engaging way.

Field-Specific Validation

Tailor validation rules for specific fields to ensure data entered meets the exact requirements for that field.

Resetting Validation States

Provide a way to reset validation states when a form is cleared or reset, maintaining form usability.

Validating File Inputs

Include validation for file inputs, checking for file size and type, if applicable.

Conclusion

Form validation is a key component of user interactions on the web. Bootstrap's validation classes and utilities, combined with HTML5 and JavaScript, offer a robust foundation for creating effective, user-friendly, and secure form validations. By implementing these techniques, you can enhance the overall user experience and ensure the integrity of the data collected through your forms.

5.3. Creating Multi-step Forms

Multi-step forms, also known as wizard forms, are a powerful way to break up the collection of user information into more manageable chunks. Bootstrap can be utilized to create an intuitive and engaging multi-step form experience.

The Concept of Multi-Step Forms

Multi-step forms divide the form-filling process into several steps, which can make complex forms less overwhelming for users and improve overall user experience.

Structuring a Multi-Step Form

In Bootstrap, a multi-step form can be structured using a combination of tabs or progress indicators for navigation and different form sections for each step.

Using Bootstrap Tabs for Navigation

Bootstrap's tab component can be used to create the navigation for a multi-step form:

```
<ul class="nav nav-tabs">

<li class="nav-item">

<a class="nav-link active" href="#step1">Step 1</a>

</li>

<!—More steps—>

</ul>

<div id="step1">

<!—Form step 1 content—>

</div>

<!—More form steps—>
```

Implementing Progress Bars

A Bootstrap progress bar can visually indicate the current step in the form process:

```
<div class="progress">

<div class="progress-bar" role="progressbar" style="width: 25%;" aria-valuenow="25" aria-valuemin="0" aria-valuemax="100"></div>

</div>
```

Managing Form State

Use JavaScript or a JavaScript library like jQuery to manage the state of the form, handling what happens when the user navigates between steps.

Validation per Step

Implement validation for each step, ensuring the user completes the current part of the form before proceeding to the next.

Dynamically Loading Form Content

For efficiency, consider dynamically loading form content for each step, especially if the form is particularly long or complex.

Handling User Input Data

Maintain user input data across different steps using JavaScript. You can store this data in variables or utilize local storage.

Transition Effects Between Steps

Enhance user experience with smooth transition effects between form steps using Bootstrap's transition classes or additional CSS and JavaScript.

Responsive Design

Ensure that your multi-step form is responsive, providing a seamless experience across different devices.

Submitting the Form

Handle the final form submission when all steps are completed. This could be a server-side submission or an AJAX request.

Incorporating Feedback Mechanisms

Provide feedback to users after each step, such as confirmation messages or error alerts.

Customizing the Look and Feel

Customize the appearance of each step to align with the overall design of your site and to make the form more engaging.

Saving Form Progress

Consider allowing users to save their progress in multi-step forms, especially if the forms are long.

Clear Navigation and Instructions

Ensure that the form navigation is clear and provide instructions where necessary to guide users through the process.

Error Handling

Implement robust error handling, especially at the transition points between steps, to ensure a smooth user experience.

Accessibility

Ensure your multi-step form is accessible, with proper labeling and keyboard navigation.

Conclusion

Multi-step forms, when designed and implemented thoughtfully, can significantly enhance the user experience for complex data collection tasks. Bootstrap provides the necessary components and utilities to create these forms, but attention to detail in terms of validation, user feedback, and state management is key to making them effective and user-friendly.

5.4. Custom Form Controls

Custom form controls in Bootstrap allow for enhanced user interaction and better integration with the overall design theme. By customizing form elements, you can create a more cohesive and branded user experience.

Understanding Custom Form Controls

Custom form controls are modified versions of standard HTML form elements. They can be styled to match your website's design and offer improved user interaction.

Styling Text Inputs

Text inputs are the most common form elements. Customize their appearance to fit your design, while ensuring usability and accessibility:

```
<input type of="text" class="form-control custom-text-input">
```

Customizing Checkboxes and Radios

Bootstrap provides a way to create custom checkboxes and radio buttons that are more visually appealing than the default browser styles:

```
<div class="custom-control custom-checkbox">

<input type="checkbox" class="custom-control-input" id="customCheck">
```

```
<label class="custom-control-label" for="customCheck">Check this custom checkbox</label>

</div>
```

Styling Select Menus

Select menus can be customized for a more consistent look across different browsers and platforms:

```
<select class="custom-select">

<option selected>Open this select menu</option>

<!—Options—>

</select>
```

Creating Toggle Switches

Toggle switches are a modern alternative to checkboxes. Use Bootstrap's custom switch control for a more engaging UI:

```
<div class="custom-control custom-switch">

<input type="checkbox" class="custom-control-input" id="customSwitch">

<label class="custom-control-label" for="customSwitch">Toggle this switch element</label>

</div>
```

Custom File Input

Styling file inputs can be challenging due to browser limitations, but Bootstrap provides custom styles that can be further tailored:

```
<div class="custom-file">

<input type="file" class="custom-file-input" id="customFile">

<label class="custom-file-label" for="customFile">Choose file</label>

</div>
```

Range Inputs

Customize range inputs (sliders) with Bootstrap for a consistent and improved user experience:

```
<input type="range" class="custom-range" id="customRange">
```

Handling Focus and Hover States

Ensure that custom form controls have clearly defined focus and hover states to enhance usability.

Integrating with JavaScript

For more advanced functionalities like date pickers or color selectors, integrate your custom form controls with JavaScript plugins or libraries.

Responsive Design

Make sure your custom form controls are responsive, ensuring they work well on different devices and screen sizes.

Theming Form Controls

Align the design of your form controls with your site's theme, using consistent colors, borders, and typography.

Accessibility Considerations

Ensure custom form controls are accessible, with proper labeling and keyboard navigation support.

Validating Custom Controls

Implement validation styles for custom controls to provide feedback on user input.

Dynamic Form Controls

Consider adding functionality to dynamically add or remove form controls based on user actions.

Performance

Optimize for performance by minimizing additional HTML, CSS, and JavaScript used for custom form controls.

Testing Across Browsers and Devices

Test your custom form controls across different browsers and devices to ensure consistent behavior and appearance.

Conclusion

Custom form controls in Bootstrap enhance the user experience by providing a consistent and visually appealing interface. By carefully designing these controls, you can ensure that they not only look good but also remain functional and accessible across various devices and browsers.

5.5. Accessibility in Forms

Ensuring accessibility in forms is crucial for creating an inclusive web experience. Bootstrap provides various features and best practices that can be utilized to make forms accessible to all users, including those with disabilities.

Understanding the Importance of Accessible Forms

Accessible forms are essential for users with disabilities to interact with your website. This includes users who rely on screen readers, keyboard navigation, and other assistive technologies.

Using Semantic HTML

Use semantic HTML elements for form structure, as they provide built-in accessibility features. For example, use <form>, <input>, <label>, and <button> tags in their appropriate context.

Labeling Form Elements

Ensure that all form elements have proper labels. The <label> tag associates text with form elements, which is crucial for screen reader users:

```
<label for="inputEmail">Email address</label>

<input type of="email" id="inputEmail" class="form-control">
```

Placeholder Text and Accessibility

While placeholder text can provide hints, it should not replace labels, as it can be missed by screen readers and can disappear when users start typing.

Indicating Required Fields

Clearly indicate required fields, either with text (e.g., "Required") or symbols. However, ensure that these indicators are also accessible to screen reader users.

Error Identification and Description

Provide clear error identification and descriptive messages that can help users easily rectify mistakes in form input.

Accessible Form Validation

Implement accessible form validation that provides users with clear feedback. Use ARIA roles and properties to enhance the experience for screen reader users.

Keyboard Navigation

Ensure that all form elements are navigable with a keyboard. This includes form fields, checkboxes, radio buttons, and custom controls.

Focus Management

Manage focus appropriately in forms, especially in multi-step forms or modal dialogs. The focus should move logically through form elements.

Using ARIA Roles and Attributes

Use ARIA roles and attributes where necessary to provide additional context to assistive technologies. For example, aria-invalid="true" can be used to indicate an invalid field.

Accessible File Uploads

For file upload inputs, provide clear instructions and ensure that the control is accessible with assistive technologies.

Custom Controls and Accessibility

If you are using custom form controls, ensure that they are fully accessible, including proper keyboard navigation and screen reader support.

Contrast and Visibility

Maintain high contrast between text and background colors to ensure readability for users with visual impairments.

Responsive and Accessible Forms

Design your forms to be both responsive and accessible, ensuring they work well on mobile devices and screen readers.

Testing for Accessibility

Regularly test your forms for accessibility using tools like screen readers, keyboard navigation, and accessibility audit tools.

Training and Awareness

Educate your team about the importance of accessible forms. Promote a culture where accessibility is a key part of the development process.

Conclusion

Accessibility in forms is a vital aspect of web development that should not be overlooked. By following these guidelines and utilizing Bootstrap's features, you can create forms that are accessible to all users, ensuring an inclusive web experience.

Chapter 6: Bootstrap and JavaScript

6.1. JavaScript Components Overview

Bootstrap, renowned for its responsive design capabilities, also boasts an impressive collection of JavaScript components. These components provide interactivity and dynamic functionalities to web pages, enhancing user experience significantly.

JavaScript in Bootstrap is primarily used to manipulate DOM elements, handle events, and add dynamic content. The beauty of Bootstrap's JavaScript components lies in their simplicity and ease of integration with HTML elements.

The Essence of Data Attributes

Bootstrap's JavaScript components heavily rely on data attributes. These attributes allow you to add JavaScript functionalities to HTML elements without writing any JavaScript code. For example, adding data-toggle="modal" to a button element binds a click event to it, triggering a modal pop-up.

Utilizing jQuery and Vanilla JavaScript

While Bootstrap 5 has moved away from jQuery, offering a more modern approach using plain JavaScript (also known as Vanilla JavaScript), understanding how Bootstrap previously interacted with jQuery can be beneficial for developers working on projects that use older versions of Bootstrap.

Modal Component

The Modal component is a classic example, used for creating dialog boxes, popups, and custom overlays. It can be triggered using JavaScript like so:

```
var myModal = new bootstrap.Modal(document.getElementById('myModal'), options)

myModal.show()
```

This code snippet demonstrates the instantiation of a modal and then displaying it.

Tooltip and Popover

Tooltips and popovers provide contextual information to users. They are triggered on specific actions like hover or focus. In Bootstrap 5, these can be easily implemented:

```
var tooltipTriggerList = [].slice.call(document.querySelectorAll('[data-bs-toggle="tooltip"]'))

var tooltipList = tooltipTriggerList.map(function (tooltipTriggerEl) {

return new bootstrap.Tooltip(tooltipTriggerEl)

})
```

This code enables tooltips on all elements with the data-bs-toggle="tooltip" attribute.

Collapse Component

The Collapse component is useful for toggling the visibility of content. It's commonly used for accordions and navbar toggles in responsive layouts. Implementing it is straightforward:

```
var myCollapse = document.getElementById('myCollapse')

var bsCollapse = new bootstrap.Collapse(myCollapse, {

toggle: false

})
```

The Carousel Component

A carousel is a slideshow component for cycling through elements, typically images or slides of text. It can be controlled via JavaScript as follows:

```
var myCarousel = document.getElementById('myCarousel')

var carousel = new bootstrap.Carousel(myCarousel, {

interval: 2000,

wrap: false

})
```

Tabs and Pills

For content organization, Bootstrap offers Tabs and Pills, which can be manipulated via JavaScript to dynamically show or hide content sections.

Alerts

Bootstrap provides an alert component that can be dismissed by the user. JavaScript is used to remove the alert from the DOM.

Dynamic Behaviors

JavaScript components in Bootstrap can be dynamically added or removed from the DOM. This is particularly useful in single-page applications where the DOM elements are not all present from the start.

Event Handling

Bootstrap's JavaScript components emit various custom events for different lifecycle stages. For example, modals have events like show.bs.modal, shown.bs.modal, hide.bs.modal, and hidden.bs.modal. Listening to these events allows for the execution of custom code in response to component interactions.

Customizing Components

Developers can extend the functionality of Bootstrap's JavaScript components or customize them to suit specific needs. This could involve modifying the default options or writing new methods.

Performance Considerations

While adding interactivity, it's crucial to consider the performance implications. Overuse of JavaScript or improper use of components can lead to sluggish performance, particularly on mobile devices.

In conclusion, Bootstrap's JavaScript components are a robust set of tools that enhance the interactivity and functionality of web pages. By understanding how to effectively use and customize these components, developers can create more engaging and dynamic user experiences.

6.2. Interactive Components: Tooltips and Popovers

Tooltips and popovers in Bootstrap are essential for enhancing user interfaces by providing contextual or supplementary information. These interactive components are not just aesthetically pleasing but also aid in improving user experience by offering necessary details without cluttering the UI.

Tooltips: A Closer Look

Tooltips are small, interactive text boxes that appear when the user hovers over or focuses on an element. They are used to provide additional information about a button, link, or any other user interface element.

Implementing Tooltips

To add a tooltip, you simply use a data attribute like data-bs-toggle="tooltip" and a title attribute for the text. Bootstrap's JavaScript then takes care of the rest. Here's an example:

```
<button type="button" class="btn btn-secondary" data-bs-toggle="tooltip" data-bs-placement="top" title="Tooltip on top">

Tooltip on top

</button>
```

Popovers: Providing More Content

Popovers are similar to tooltips but are capable of displaying more content - this can include text and HTML. They're perfect for situations where more extensive explanations or information is required.

Creating Popovers

Implementing a popover is as straightforward as implementing a tooltip. You use the data-bs-toggle="popover" attribute. Popovers can contain both a title and content, which can be specified in the attributes. Here's a sample implementation:

```
<button type="button" class="btn btn-lg btn-danger" data-bs-toggle="popover" title="Popover title" data-bs-content="And here's some amazing content. It's very engaging. Right?">Click to toggle popover</button>
```

Customizing Display

Both tooltips and popovers come with options for customization. You can control their positioning (top, bottom, left, right), trigger events (click, hover, focus), and even HTML content for popovers.

JavaScript Customization

For more dynamic control, these components can be initialized and customized using JavaScript. For example, you can change the trigger event or animation:

```
var popover = new bootstrap.Popover(document.querySelector('.popover-dismiss'), {
```

```
trigger: 'focus'

})
```

Handling Events

Bootstrap emits events for tooltips and popovers, like show.bs.tooltip, shown.bs.tooltip, hide.bs.tooltip, hidden.bs.tooltip, and their popover equivalents. These can be used to execute custom code:

```
document.getElementById('myPopover').addEventListener('hidden.bs.p
function () {

// Code to execute after popover is hidden

})
```

Responsiveness and Positioning

Bootstrap automatically handles the responsiveness of these components. However, in complex layouts, you might need to manually control the positioning to ensure they don't overflow the viewport.

Accessibility Considerations

When using tooltips and popovers, it's crucial to consider accessibility. Ensure that these components are accessible through keyboard navigation and screen readers. Use the aria-describedby attribute for tooltips and aria-labelledby for popovers when necessary.

Performance Tips

While tooltips and popovers add interactivity, they should be used judiciously. Overuse can impact performance, especially on mobile devices or low-powered devices.

Custom Themes

The look and feel of tooltips and popovers can be customized to match your application's theme. This includes colors, fonts, and borders, which can be customized via CSS or SASS variables.

Lazy Loading

For performance optimization, especially in a web application with many tooltips or popovers, consider implementing lazy loading. This means initializing these components only when they are needed.

Interactive Content

Popovers can house interactive content, such as links or buttons. This feature can be leveraged to create mini-menus or additional user interactions within a popover.

Security Considerations

When enabling HTML content inside popovers, be cautious of security risks like XSS attacks. Always sanitize the content to prevent the injection of malicious scripts.

Destroying Tooltips and Popovers

To free up resources, you can programmatically destroy tooltips or popovers when they are no longer needed. This is particularly useful in single-page applications where DOM elements are frequently created and removed.

Best Practices

Always test tooltips and popovers across different devices and browsers to ensure consistent behavior. Also, keep the content concise and relevant.

In conclusion, tooltips and popovers in Bootstrap offer a powerful way to enhance user interfaces with additional information and interactivity. With proper implementation and customization, they can significantly improve the usability and aesthetic appeal of web applications.

6.3. Dynamic Modals and Alerts

Bootstrap's dynamic modals and alerts are powerful tools for engaging with users, displaying information, and gathering input in a responsive and interactive manner. These components are essential for modern web applications, offering a variety of uses from user notifications to form submissions.

Understanding Modals

Modals in Bootstrap are essentially dialog boxes or pop-up windows that are displayed over the main content. They can be used for various purposes, such as collecting user input, confirming actions, or displaying information.

Creating a Modal

A basic modal in Bootstrap requires HTML for the structure, CSS for styling, and JavaScript for functionality. Here's a simple example:

```
<!—Modal Trigger Button—>

<button type="button" class="btn btn-primary" data-bs-toggle="modal" data-bs-target="#exampleModal">

Launch demo modal

</button>

<!—Modal Structure—>

<div class="modal fade" id="exampleModal" tabindex="-1" aria-labelledby="exampleModalLabel" aria-hidden="true">

<div class="modal-dialog">

<div class="modal-content">

<div class="modal-header">

<h5 class="modal-title" id="exampleModalLabel">Modal title</h5>

<button type="button" class="btn-close" data-bs-dismiss="modal" aria-label="Close"></button>

</div>

<div class="modal-body">

Your content here.

</div>

<div class="modal-footer">

<button type="button" class="btn btn-secondary" data-bs-dismiss="modal">Close</button>
```

```
<button type="button" class="btn btn-primary">Save changes</button>

</div>

</div>

</div>

</div>
```

JavaScript Control of Modals

Modals can be controlled programmatically using JavaScript. This is particularly useful for showing or hiding a modal based on specific conditions or events:

```
var myModal = new bootstrap.Modal(document.getElementById('myModal'));

myModal.show(); // To show the modal

myModal.hide(); // To hide the modal
```

Events in Modals

Bootstrap modals emit events for each stage in their lifecycle, such as show.bs.modal, shown.bs.modal, hide.bs.modal, and hidden.bs.modal. These can be used to execute code at specific points:

```
$('#myModal').on('hidden.bs.modal', function (e) {

// Code to run after modal has been hidden

})
```

Customizing Modals

Modals are highly customizable. You can change their size, transition effects, and even include various forms of content, including forms, images, and videos.

Accessibility in Modals

Ensuring modals are accessible is crucial. This includes proper keyboard navigation, screen reader support, and focus management. Bootstrap's modals are designed with accessibility in mind, but developers should ensure that additional content within modals also meets accessibility standards.

Implementing Alerts

Alerts are used to convey messages to users, typically for success, warning, or error information. They are simple to implement and can be automatically dismissed or require user interaction to close.

Creating an Alert

A basic alert in Bootstrap looks like this:

```
<div class="alert alert-warning alert-dismissible fade show" role="alert">

<strong>Holy guacamole!</strong> You should check in on some of those fields below.

<button type="button" class="btn-close" data-bs-dismiss="alert" aria-label="Close"></button>

</div>
```

Dynamic Behavior of Alerts

Alerts can be made dynamic by controlling them with JavaScript. For instance, an alert can be triggered by an event, such as the completion of a form submission.

Customizing Alerts

Bootstrap alerts can be customized in terms of color, size, and content. They can also be animated to fade in and out.

Dismissing Alerts with JavaScript

JavaScript can be used to programmatically dismiss alerts:

```
var alertPlaceholder = document.getElementById('liveAlertPlaceholder')

var alertTrigger = document.getElementById('liveAlertBtn')

function alert(message, type) {

var wrapper = document.createElement('div')

wrapper.innerHTML = '<div class="alert alert-' + type + ' alert-dismissible" role="alert">' + message + '</div>'

alertPlaceholder.append(wrapper)

}

if (alertTrigger) {

alertTrigger.addEventListener('click', function () {

alert('Nice, you triggered this alert message!', 'success')

})
```

```
}
```

Handling Events in Alerts

Alerts in Bootstrap can also emit events, similar to modals. This allows for actions to be taken when an alert is shown or hidden.

Performance Considerations

While alerts and modals enhance interactivity, it's important to use them judiciously to avoid overloading the user and to maintain optimal performance, especially on mobile devices.

Best Practices

When using modals and alerts, always consider the user experience. Ensure that

---

6.4. Integrating with JavaScript Frameworks

Integrating Bootstrap with various JavaScript frameworks enhances its capabilities, allowing for more dynamic and responsive web applications. Each framework, with its unique features, complements Bootstrap's components, offering a more robust development experience.

Understanding Framework Integration

Integrating Bootstrap with JavaScript frameworks like Angular, React, or Vue.js involves understanding how Bootstrap's styling and components work within the framework's ecosystem. This includes manipulating the DOM, handling state, and reacting to user events.

Angular Integration

Angular, a TypeScript-based framework, is known for its powerful data-binding and dependency injection. Integrating Bootstrap with Angular often involves using specialized libraries like ng-bootstrap or ngx-bootstrap, which provide Bootstrap components as native Angular directives and services.

```
import { NgbModule } from '@ng-bootstrap/ng-bootstrap';

@NgModule({

...

imports: [NgbModule, ...],

...

})

export class YourAppModule { }
```

React Integration

React's component-based architecture makes it a great match for Bootstrap. Libraries like react-bootstrap repackage Bootstrap components as React components, ensuring compatibility and ease of use.

```
import { Button } from 'react-bootstrap';

const ExampleComponent = () => {

return <Button variant="primary">Click me</Button>;

};
```

Vue.js Integration

Vue.js, known for its simplicity and progressive nature, can be integrated with Bootstrap using libraries like bootstrap-vue that offer Bootstrap components as Vue components.

```
<template>

<b-button variant="success">Click Me</b-button>

</template>

<script>

import { BButton } from 'bootstrap-vue';

export default {

components: {

BButton

}

};

</script>
```

Handling State and Events

When integrating Bootstrap with these frameworks, handling state and events becomes crucial. For instance, showing or hiding a modal in React might involve changing a component's state.

Customizing Components

Customizing Bootstrap components to fit within a framework's architecture might require overriding styles or extending components with additional properties and methods.

Form Handling

Integrating Bootstrap forms with JavaScript frameworks enhances their functionality, allowing for more complex form validation and submission processes.

Routing and Navigation

Frameworks like Angular and React come with their routing solutions. Integrating Bootstrap's navigational components with these routing mechanisms is key for creating SPA (Single Page Application) experiences.

Performance Optimization

Each framework has its way of optimizing performance, and it's essential to align these with Bootstrap's components to ensure a smooth user experience.

State Management

Complex applications might require state management solutions like Redux (for React) or Vuex (for Vue.js). It's important to understand how these state management tools interact with Bootstrap components.

Accessibility Considerations

Ensuring accessibility when integrating Bootstrap with JavaScript frameworks is crucial. This involves managing focus, keyboard navigation, and ARIA attributes.

Responsive Design

Bootstrap's responsive design capabilities need to be harmoniously integrated with the framework's responsive handling, ensuring a consistent experience across devices.

Server-Side Rendering (SSR)

Frameworks like React and Vue.js support SSR, which can be crucial for SEO and performance. Integrating Bootstrap in SSR scenarios requires understanding how the framework handles server-side and client-side rendering.

Event Delegation

Understanding how each framework handles events is crucial, especially when working with Bootstrap components that rely on JavaScript for functionality.

Theming and Styling

Customizing the look and feel of Bootstrap components within a framework can involve using the framework's styling conventions, such as styled-components in React or scoped styles in Vue.js.

Dynamic Component Loading

Leveraging the dynamic component loading capabilities of these frameworks can enhance the performance and user experience of applications using Bootstrap components.

Best Practices

Following best practices for each framework, such as proper component structuring in React or efficient data handling in Angular, ensures a robust and maintainable codebase when integrated with Bootstrap.

Community and Resources

Leveraging the community and resources available for each framework, including official documentation and third-party tutorials, is key to successful integration with Bootstrap.

Integrating Bootstrap with JavaScript frameworks unlocks a world of possibilities, allowing developers to create more dynamic, responsive, and user-friendly web applications. By understanding the nuances of each framework and how they interact with Bootstrap, developers can build sophisticated and efficient web applications.

6.5. Performance Optimization

Performance optimization is crucial in web development, ensuring that applications are not only functional and aesthetically pleasing but also efficient and responsive. When integrating Bootstrap with JavaScript, several strategies can be employed to enhance performance.

Understanding the Impact of JavaScript

JavaScript, especially when used extensively for dynamic components and interactivity, can significantly affect a website's performance. Minimizing and optimizing JavaScript usage is key to maintaining fast load times and smooth interactions.

Minimizing JavaScript

One of the first steps in performance optimization is to minimize the amount of JavaScript used. This involves using only the necessary Bootstrap components and not loading entire libraries when only a few functions are needed.

Efficient DOM Manipulation

DOM manipulation can be costly in terms of performance. Optimizing how Bootstrap interacts with the DOM, such as minimizing reflows and repaints, can lead to better performance.

Example of Efficient DOM Updates

When updating the DOM, batch changes together to minimize reflows. For instance, if you're adding multiple Bootstrap cards dynamically, append them as a group rather than one by one.

Asynchronous Loading

Loading JavaScript asynchronously ensures that it does not block the rendering of the page. This can be done using the async or defer attributes in script tags.

Implementing Async Loading

Here's an example of loading the Bootstrap JavaScript file asynchronously:

```
<script src="path/to/bootstrap.js" async></script>
```

Utilizing Browser Caching

Leveraging browser caching for Bootstrap's JavaScript files reduces load times for repeat visitors. This can be configured via server settings or by using service workers.

Compressing and Minifying Files

Compressing and minifying JavaScript files reduces their size, leading to faster download times. Tools like UglifyJS or Terser can be used for minification.

Example of JavaScript Minification

Using a build tool like Webpack or Gulp, you can set up a process to automatically minify your Bootstrap JavaScript files as part of your build process.

Using Content Delivery Networks (CDNs)

Serving Bootstrap's JavaScript files from a CDN can improve load times due to reduced latency and enhanced caching.

Eliminating Render-Blocking JavaScript

Identifying and eliminating render-blocking JavaScript, especially during the initial page load, can significantly improve performance.

This might involve restructuring how scripts are loaded or using inline scripts for critical functionalities.

Lazy Loading Components

Lazy loading Bootstrap components that are not immediately needed can enhance performance, especially for content below the fold.

Example of Lazy Loading

Using Intersection Observer API, you can detect when a Bootstrap carousel enters the viewport and then dynamically load it.

Debouncing and Throttling

Debouncing and throttling event handlers, especially for events that fire frequently like resize or scroll, can prevent excessive JavaScript execution and improve performance.

Debouncing Example

```
function debounce(func, wait, immediate) {
var timeout;
return function() {
var context = this, args = arguments;
clearTimeout(timeout);
timeout = setTimeout(function() {
timeout = null;
```

```
if (!immediate) func.apply(context, args);

}, wait);

if (immediate && !timeout) func.apply(context, args);

};

};

window.addEventListener('resize', debounce(function() {

// Code to execute after resize, with controlled frequency

}, 250));
```

Optimizing for Mobile Devices

Considering mobile devices' limitations in terms of processing power and bandwidth is essential. This includes responsive design, touch event optimization, and minimizing heavy computations.

Monitoring Performance

Regularly monitoring the performance of your Bootstrap-enhanced website using tools like Google PageSpeed Insights, Lighthouse, or Chrome DevTools is essential to identify and address performance issues.

Best Practices

Adhering to best practices in JavaScript and Bootstrap implementation, such as avoiding inline styles, using semantic HTML, and following progressive enhancement principles, contributes significantly to performance optimization.

Optimizing performance when using Bootstrap and JavaScript is a continuous process that involves various techniques and best practices. By focusing on efficient code, minimizing resource usage, and regularly monitoring performance, developers can ensure that their web applications are not only visually appealing and functional but also fast and responsive.

Chapter 7: Responsive Web Design

7.1. Mobile-First Approach

The mobile-first approach in web design prioritizes optimizing websites for mobile devices before making adjustments for larger screens. This strategy is particularly relevant in the current digital landscape where mobile usage often surpasses desktop usage.

The Concept of Mobile-First Design

Mobile-first design involves starting the design process with the mobile experience as the primary focus, and then scaling up to larger screens. This approach ensures that websites are inherently mobile-friendly and accessible.

Key Characteristics of Mobile-First Design

- Simplified designs focusing on essential content.
- Streamlined navigation to accommodate smaller screens.
- Prioritizing performance for slower mobile networks.

Implementing Mobile-First with Bootstrap

Bootstrap, with its responsive grid system and mobile-first philosophy, provides an excellent framework for implementing a mobile-first design.

Example of Mobile-First Grid

```
<div class="container">
<div class="row">
<div class="col-12 col-md-8">Main Content</div>
<div class="col-12 col-md-4">Sidebar</div>
</div>
</div>
```

In this example, the col-12 class ensures full-width columns on mobile, while col-md-8 and col-md-4 adjust the layout for larger screens.

Importance of Responsive Images

Responsive images are crucial in a mobile-first design. They adapt in size and resolution to different screen sizes and resolutions, ensuring optimal loading times and display quality.

Implementing Responsive Images in Bootstrap

```
<img src="image.jpg" class="img-fluid" alt="Responsive image">
```

The img-fluid class in Bootstrap makes the image responsive, allowing it to scale with the size of its container.

Typography and Readability

Typography plays a significant role in mobile-first design. Ensuring text is readable on small screens without zooming is crucial for a positive user experience.

Responsive Typography

Using relative units like em or rem for font sizes and line heights helps maintain readability across devices.

Touch Targets and Interactivity

On mobile devices, designing larger touch targets for buttons and links is essential for usability. Bootstrap's built-in padding and margin classes can be used to enhance touch targets.

Example of Enhancing Touch Targets

```
<button class="btn btn-primary btn-lg">Large Button</button>
```

The btn-lg class in Bootstrap increases the size of the button, making it easier to tap on mobile.

Simplifying Navigation

Mobile-first design often involves simplifying navigation structures. Complex multi-level menus are replaced with dropdowns or off-canvas menus to conserve space and improve usability.

Implementing Simplified Navigation in Bootstrap

Using Bootstrap's navbar component with the navbar-expand-* classes allows for collapsible menus at specified breakpoints.

Optimizing Forms for Mobile

Forms should be designed with mobile users in mind, minimizing the required input and ensuring easy usability.

Mobile-Friendly Forms

Arranging form fields vertically and using input types like date, email, and number enhances mobile usability.

Performance Optimization

In a mobile-first approach, optimizing for performance is crucial. This includes minimizing file sizes, compressing images, and reducing the use of heavy JavaScript.

Testing on Real Devices

While simulators and emulators are useful, testing on actual mobile devices provides the most accurate representation of the user experience.

Continuous Adaptation

Mobile-first design is not a one-time task but a continuous process. Regular updates and optimizations based on user feedback and analytics are essential.

Accessibility Considerations

Ensuring that mobile designs are accessible to all users, including those with disabilities, is a key aspect of the mobile-first approach.

In conclusion, the mobile-first approach in responsive web design is about starting with the smallest screen and then scaling up. It ensures that websites are optimized for mobile devices first, which is crucial in today's mobile-dominated internet usage. Bootstrap's framework supports this approach effectively, providing tools and components that make implementing mobile-first designs more straightforward and efficient.

7.2. Media Queries and Responsive Utilities

Media queries are foundational to responsive web design, allowing CSS to adapt to different screen sizes, resolutions, and orientations. Bootstrap's responsive utilities leverage these media queries to create layouts that respond to various device characteristics.

Understanding Media Queries

Media queries enable the application of CSS styles based on media type (like screen) and specific characteristics (such as width, height, or orientation). They are the key mechanism behind responsive design.

Basic Syntax of Media Queries

```
@media (min-width: 768px) {

.example-class {

background-color: blue;

}

}
```

This media query applies the background color style to .example-class when the viewport width is 768 pixels or more.

Bootstrap's Breakpoints

Bootstrap defines a set of breakpoints for various device sizes, such as extra small (xs), small (sm), medium (md), large (lg), and extra large (xl). These predefined breakpoints simplify the process of designing for multiple screens.

Utilizing Bootstrap Breakpoints

```
<div class="col-md-6 col-lg-4"></div>
```

In this example, the column takes up half the container on medium devices and a third on large devices, thanks to Bootstrap's grid system.

Responsive Typography

Typography should be responsive, adapting to screen size for optimal readability. Bootstrap provides utility classes for responsive text alignment, wrapping, and resizing.

Example of Responsive Typography

```
<h1 class="display-4">Large Heading</h1>

<p class="lead">This is a lead paragraph.</p>
```

These classes style the text size and weight appropriate for different devices.

Responsive Images

Images in a responsive layout need to adapt to different screen sizes without losing clarity or causing layout issues.

Making Images Responsive in Bootstrap

```
<img src="image.jpg" class="img-fluid" alt="Responsive image">
```

The img-fluid class ensures that the image scales with its container.

Responsive Visibility

Bootstrap includes utility classes to show or hide elements based on the screen size. This is useful for optimizing content for different devices.

Example of Responsive Visibility

```
<div class="d-none d-md-block">Visible on medium and larger screens</div>
```

This element will be hidden on small screens and visible on medium and larger screens.

Mobile-First and Desktop-First Strategies

Media queries can be used in a mobile-first (min-width) or desktop-first (max-width) approach. Bootstrap uses a mobile-first approach, which is generally recommended for modern web design.

Custom Media Queries

Besides Bootstrap's predefined breakpoints, custom media queries can be written to target specific devices or conditions.

Custom Media Query Example

```
@media (max-width: 600px) {

.custom-class {

padding: 20px;

}

}
```

This custom media query adds padding to .custom-class on screens smaller than 600px.

Responsive Margins and Padding

Bootstrap provides responsive spacing classes that adjust margins and padding based on the viewport size.

Example of Responsive Spacing

```
<div class="mt-2 mt-md-4">Content</div>
```

This sets a top margin of 2 on all sizes and increases it to 4 on medium and larger devices.

Flexbox and CSS Grid

Utilizing Flexbox and CSS Grid with media queries provides powerful layout options that are responsive and adaptable.

Flexbox with Media Queries

```
@media (min-width: 768px) {

.container {

display: flex;

}

}
```

In this example, the container uses Flexbox on wider screens.

Responsive Tables

Tables can be made responsive with Bootstrap's .table-responsive class, which makes them scroll horizontally on small devices.

Making a Table Responsive

```
<div class="table-responsive">

<table class="table">

<!—Table content—>

</table>

</div>
```

Responsive Utilities for Layout

Bootstrap's layout utilities, like w-100 (width 100%) and h-auto (auto height), are helpful in creating responsive designs.

Testing and Debugging

It's important to test responsive designs across various devices and viewports to ensure consistency and usability.

In summary, media queries and responsive utilities are essential tools in creating web designs that adapt to different screen sizes and orientations. Bootstrap offers a comprehensive set of utilities and components to facilitate responsive design, making it easier for developers to create websites that offer optimal user experiences on any device.

7.3. Optimizing Layouts for Different

Devices

Optimizing web layouts for different devices is a critical aspect of responsive web design. It involves ensuring that the content and design adapt seamlessly across a range of devices, from mobile phones to large desktop screens.

Responsive Grid System

Bootstrap's grid system is a cornerstone of responsive layout design. It uses a series of containers, rows, and columns to layout and align content in a flexible and responsive manner.

Example of a Responsive Grid

```
<div class="container">

<div class="row">

<div class="col-sm-12 col-md-6 col-lg-4">Content here</div>

<div class="col-sm-12 col-md-6 col-lg-4">Content here</div>

<div class="col-sm-12 col-md-6 col-lg-4">Content here</div>

</div>

</div>
```

In this setup, the layout adjusts from a single column on small devices to two columns on medium devices, and three columns on large devices.

Fluid Containers

Using fluid containers allows the layout to adapt to the width of the viewport. This is essential for creating a layout that stretches across different screen sizes.

Implementing Fluid Layout

```
<div class="container-fluid">
<!—Content here will stretch to the width of the viewport—>
</div>
```

Responsive Images

Ensuring that images resize and fit well in the layout across devices is vital. Bootstrap's responsive image class .img-fluid makes an image scale nicely to the parent element.

Typography Adjustments

Typography should also be responsive. Font sizes, line heights, and even font weights may need to change based on the device to ensure readability and aesthetics.

CSS for Responsive Typography

```
@media (max-width: 600px) {
h1 {
font-size: 24px;
}
```

```
}
```

In this example, the h1 font size decreases for devices with a width of 600px or less.

Handling Tables Responsively

Tables can be challenging in responsive design due to their tabular nature. Bootstrap's .table-responsive class allows tables to be scrolled horizontally on small devices.

Collapsible Menus and Accordions

On smaller screens, navigation menus and large blocks of content can be transformed into collapsible elements or accordions to save space.

Creating a Collapsible Menu

```
<div class="collapse" id="navbarToggleExternalContent">

<div class="bg-dark p-4">

<!—Collapsible content—>

</div>

</div>
```

Modal and Overlay Adjustments

Modals and overlays should be carefully handled to ensure they fit and function well on small screens.

Hidden and Visible Utility Classes

Bootstrap's utility classes for visibility (d-none, d-*-block) allow for showing or hiding elements based on the screen size.

Responsive Padding and Margin

Adjusting padding and margins responsively can greatly enhance the layout's appearance and usability across devices.

Responsive Spacing in Bootstrap

```
<div class="m-2 m-md-4">Content</div>
```

This sets different margins for medium and larger devices.

Responsive Flexbox and CSS Grid

Leveraging Flexbox and CSS Grid with Bootstrap's responsive utilities provides powerful and flexible layout options.

Optimizing Forms for Mobile

Forms should be easy to fill out on mobile devices. Larger form controls, simplified layouts, and clear labels are key.

Testing Across Devices

Regular testing on actual devices, or using device emulators, ensures that the layout performs well across different screen sizes and orientations.

Performance Considerations

While designing for different devices, it's crucial to keep performance in mind. This includes optimizing images, minifying CSS and JavaScript, and reducing HTTP requests.

Accessibility in Responsive Design

Ensure that the design remains accessible across devices. This includes readable font sizes, sufficient contrast, and accessible navigation.

User Experience Focus

Throughout the design process, keep the user experience at the forefront. Responsive design should not only be about aesthetic adaptation but also about functional and usability improvements.

In summary, optimizing layouts for different devices requires a careful balance of flexibility, usability, and aesthetics. Bootstrap provides a robust foundation with its responsive grid system and utility classes, but careful planning and testing are key to creating an optimal user experience across all devices.

7.4. Accessibility and SEO Best Practices

Accessibility and Search Engine Optimization (SEO) are vital components of web design, ensuring that websites are usable by everyone, including people with disabilities, and are easily discoverable by search engines. Integrating these practices into responsive web design is essential for creating inclusive and effective websites.

Understanding Web Accessibility

Web accessibility involves designing and developing websites so that people with disabilities can use them. This includes screen reader compatibility, keyboard navigation, and content that is accessible to all.

Accessibility Features in Bootstrap

Bootstrap includes features like ARIA attributes and semantic HTML to enhance accessibility. It's crucial to use these features correctly to make your website more accessible.

Semantic HTML for Accessibility and SEO

Using semantic HTML tags like <header>, <nav>, <main>, <footer>, and <article> improves both accessibility and SEO. These tags provide meaning to the content, aiding in navigation for screen readers and search engine crawlers.

Example of Semantic HTML

```
<main role="main">

<article>

<h1>Article Title</h1>

<p>Article content...</p>

</article>

</main>
```

Alt Text for Images

Providing descriptive alt text for images is crucial for screen readers and also benefits SEO by allowing search engines to understand the content of images.

Implementing Alt Text in Bootstrap

```
<img src="image.jpg" class="img-fluid" alt="Descriptive text about the image">
```

Keyboard Navigation

Ensure that all interactive elements are accessible via keyboard. This includes using focusable elements like buttons and links and avoiding custom elements that can't be focused or operated with a keyboard.

Color Contrast and Readability

Maintaining high contrast between text and background colors is important for readability, especially for users with visual impairments. Tools like WebAIM's Contrast Checker can be used to test color contrast.

SEO-Friendly URLs

Use clear, descriptive URLs that reflect the content of the page. This aids in SEO and helps users understand the structure of your website.

Responsive Design and Mobile SEO

Since search engines like Google prioritize mobile-friendly sites, ensuring that your responsive design works well on mobile devices is critical for SEO.

Mobile SEO Practices

- Use a responsive layout.
- Optimize load times for mobile.
- Avoid using Flash.

Structured Data

Using structured data helps search engines better understand and index your content. Schema.org provides a framework for this data.

Example of Structured Data

```
<div itemscope itemtype="http://schema.org/Book">

<span itemprop="name">Title of the book</span>

by <span itemprop="author">Author's Name</span>

</div>
```

Meta Tags for SEO

Meta tags such as <title>, <meta name="description">, and <meta name="keywords"> provide search engines with information about the webpage's content.

Optimizing Load Time

Page load time is a factor in both SEO and user experience. Optimize images, minify CSS and JavaScript, and leverage browser caching to improve load times.

Use of Heading Tags

Correct use of heading tags (<h1> through <h6>) organizes content and aids in SEO. Ensure that there is only one <h1> tag per page and that headings are used in a hierarchical manner.

Link Building and SEO

Internal and external linking strategies enhance SEO. Use descriptive anchor text for links and ensure that all links are relevant and add value to the content.

Regular Audits and Updates

Regularly audit your website for accessibility and SEO. Tools like Google Lighthouse can provide insights and suggest improvements.

Accessibility Testing

Test your website with real users, including people with disabilities, to ensure that it is accessible. Use screen readers and other assistive technologies to test the accessibility of your website.

In conclusion, integrating accessibility and SEO best practices into responsive web design not only enhances the usability and reach of a website but also contributes to a more inclusive and effective web experience. Keeping these considerations in mind during the design and development process is crucial for building successful and responsible web applications.

7.5. Testing and Debugging Responsive Designs

Testing and debugging are critical phases in the development of responsive web designs. They ensure that your website not only looks good but also functions well across various devices and browsers.

Importance of Testing in Different Environments

Responsive designs must be tested in multiple environments to ensure compatibility. This includes different browsers, operating systems, and devices (both mobile and desktop).

Tools for Cross-Browser Testing

- BrowserStack: Offers real-time browser testing.
- CrossBrowserTesting: Allows testing across multiple browsers and devices.

Emulators and Real Device Testing

While emulators and simulators are useful for initial testing, testing on real devices provides insights into actual user experiences and interactions.

Responsive Testing in Development Tools

Most modern browsers offer responsive design testing tools in their developer tools. For example, Chrome's DevTools allows you to simulate various screen sizes and resolutions.

Using Chrome DevTools for Responsive Testing

- Open Chrome DevTools (F12 or Ctrl+Shift+I).
- Click on the 'Toggle Device Toolbar' button.
- Select a device from the dropdown or enter custom dimensions.

Automated Testing Tools

Automated testing tools can speed up the process of identifying issues in different environments. Tools like Selenium can automate browser testing.

Performance Testing

Performance is a critical aspect of responsive design, especially on mobile devices. Tools like Google's PageSpeed Insights and Lighthouse can assess the performance of your site on different devices.

Accessibility Testing

Ensure your responsive design is accessible. Tools like axe and WAVE can help identify accessibility issues.

Accessibility Testing with WAVE

- Use the WAVE browser extension.
- Navigate to your website.
- Run the tool to get a report on accessibility issues.

Visual Regression Testing

Visual regression testing tools like Percy or BackstopJS help in detecting unintended visual changes across different screen sizes.

Testing Touch Interactions

On mobile devices, test touch interactions to ensure that elements like buttons, links, and sliders are easily tappable and that touch gestures work as expected.

Debugging Layout Issues

Use CSS debugging techniques like outlining elements (* { outline: 1px solid red; }) to understand how elements are laid out on the page.

Checking Console for Errors

Regularly check the browser console for JavaScript or resource loading errors that could affect the functionality or layout of your site.

Network Conditions Testing

Test how your site performs under different network conditions, particularly slower networks, to ensure it remains usable on mobile devices.

Using A/B Testing for Layout Changes

A/B testing can be useful in determining which layouts or elements perform better in terms of user engagement and conversion.

Responsive Email Design Testing

If your project includes email templates, ensure they are also responsive. Tools like Litmus or Email on Acid can test email responsiveness across different clients and devices.

Continuous Integration and Deployment

Incorporate testing into your continuous integration and deployment pipeline to catch issues early in the development process.

Feedback from Real Users

Gather feedback from real users through beta testing or usability studies to identify issues that might not be apparent in controlled testing environments.

Documentation of Known Issues

Maintain a log of known issues and resolutions to streamline the debugging process in future development cycles.

In conclusion, comprehensive testing and debugging are integral to the development of responsive web designs. A combination of automated tools, manual testing, performance evaluation, and real user feedback is necessary to ensure that the final product is not only aesthetically pleasing but also functional, performant, and accessible across all platforms and devices.

Chapter 8: Advanced Layout Techniques

8.1. Flexbox and CSS Grid Integration

Flexbox and CSS Grid are two powerful layout systems in CSS, offering more flexibility and control compared to traditional layout techniques. Integrating these with Bootstrap enhances the capability to create complex and responsive layouts.

Understanding Flexbox

Flexbox is a one-dimensional layout method that offers a more efficient way to align and distribute space among items in a container, even when their size is unknown.

Basic Flexbox Concepts

- **Flex Container**: The element with display: flex or display: inline-flex applied.
- **Flex Item**: Direct children of the flex container.
- **Main Axis and Cross Axis**: Determines the direction flex items are laid out.

Using Flexbox in Bootstrap

Bootstrap 4 and later include flex utilities, allowing easy implementation of flexbox concepts in your layout.

Flexbox Example in Bootstrap

```
<div class="d-flex justify-content-between">

<div>Item 1</div>

<div>Item 2</div>

<div>Item 3</div>

</div>
```

This creates a flex container with items spaced between each other.

Understanding CSS Grid

CSS Grid is a two-dimensional layout system, enabling the creation of complex layouts with rows and columns.

Basic CSS Grid Concepts

- **Grid Container**: Element with display: grid or display: inline-grid.
- **Grid Item**: Direct children of the grid container.
- **Grid Line**: The dividing lines that make up the structure of the grid.
- **Grid Cell**: The space between two adjacent row and two adjacent column grid lines.

Integrating CSS Grid with Bootstrap

While Bootstrap primarily uses a flexbox-based grid system, CSS Grid can be used alongside Bootstrap for more complex layouts.

CSS Grid Example

```
<div style="display: grid; grid-template-columns: repeat(3, 1fr);">

<div>Item 1</div>

<div>Item 2</div>

<div>Item 3</div>

</div>
```

This creates a grid layout with three equal columns.

Responsive Design with Flexbox and Grid

Both Flexbox and CSS Grid offer responsive features, such as flexible sizing and media query support, which are key in responsive web design.

Responsive Grid Layout

```
.container {

display: grid;

grid-template-columns: repeat(auto-fill, minmax(200px, 1fr));

}
```

This creates a responsive grid that adjusts the number of columns based on the container width.

Alignment and Justification

Flexbox and Grid provide properties for aligning and justifying items, which is particularly useful in responsive design for controlling item placement across different screen sizes.

Nested Grids

CSS Grid allows nesting grids within grids, which is useful for creating complex layouts that are still easy to manage.

Overlapping Content with Grid

CSS Grid makes it easy to create layouts with overlapping content, something that's difficult with traditional layout methods.

Flexbox vs. CSS Grid

- **Flexbox** is generally better for controlling the layout of items in a single dimension (either row or column).
- **CSS Grid** is more suited for two-dimensional layouts where control over both rows and columns is required.

Browser Support

While most modern browsers support Flexbox and CSS Grid, it's important to consider browser compatibility, especially for older browsers.

Accessibility Considerations

Ensure that layouts created with Flexbox and Grid are accessible, with logical tab orders and screen reader support.

Performance Considerations

Complex layouts with many nested elements can impact performance, especially on less powerful devices. It's important to balance design complexity with performance.

Debugging Flexbox and Grid Layouts

Modern browser developer tools include features to visualize and debug Flexbox and Grid layouts, which is essential for troubleshooting layout issues.

Best Practices

- Use Flexbox for smaller, one-dimensional layouts and CSS Grid for larger, two-dimensional layouts.

- Keep layouts as simple as possible to maintain readability and performance.

- Test layouts across various devices and browsers to ensure consistency.

In summary, Flexbox and CSS Grid are powerful tools in a web developer's toolkit, allowing for the creation of flexible, responsive, and complex layouts. When integrated with Bootstrap, they provide an unparalleled level of control over web page layouts, making it easier to design layouts that work seamlessly across different screen sizes and devices.

8.2. Creative Backgrounds and Overlays

Creative backgrounds and overlays can significantly enhance the visual appeal of a website, adding depth, context, and emotion to the content. With Bootstrap, integrating these elements into a layout is straightforward, yet it offers a wide range of possibilities for creative expression.

Using Background Images

Background images can transform the look and feel of a section or an entire page. They should be chosen carefully to complement the content and not distract from it.

Implementing Background Images in CSS

```
.section {
background-image: url('path/to/image.jpg');
background-size: cover;
background-position: center;
}
```

This CSS code sets a full-width background image that covers the entire section.

Parallax Backgrounds

Parallax scrolling, where the background moves at a different speed than the foreground, creates an illusion of depth and can be visually engaging.

Creating a Parallax Effect

```
.parallax {
background-image: url('path/to/image.jpg');
```

background-attachment: fixed;

background-position: center;

background-repeat: no-repeat;

background-size: cover;

}

This effect is achieved by fixing the background image position during scrolling.

Gradient Backgrounds

Gradients are a subtle way to add vibrancy to a layout. CSS allows for linear or radial gradients, or a combination of multiple colors.

Example of a Linear Gradient

.gradient-background {

background: linear-gradient(to right, #ff7e5f, #feb47b);

}

This creates a smooth transition from one color to another.

Fullscreen Backgrounds

A fullscreen background image can create a striking visual impact, especially for landing pages or headers.

CSS for Fullscreen Backgrounds

.fullscreen-background {

```
background: url('path/to/image.jpg') no-repeat center center;
background-size: cover;
height: 100vh;
}
```

This sets the background to cover the entire viewport height.

Background Overlays

Adding a semi-transparent overlay over background images can improve readability of text and add a layer of depth to the design.

Implementing Background Overlays

```
.overlay {
background: rgba(0, 0, 0, 0.5); /* Black overlay with 50% opacity */
color: white;
}
```

Place this overlay div on top of the background image.

Responsive Backgrounds

Ensure that background images and overlays are responsive and adapt well to different screen sizes.

CSS Blend Modes

Blend modes can be used to create interesting visual effects by controlling how an element's background blends with the backgrounds behind it.

Example of Blend Mode

```
.blend-mode {
background-blend-mode: multiply;
}
```

This blends the element's background with the background behind it using the multiply effect.

Animated Backgrounds

Animated backgrounds, such as subtle gradients or slow-moving images, can add dynamic interest to a webpage.

Backgrounds for Content Sections

Different background styles for different content sections can help to visually separate and organize information on the page.

Balancing Performance and Aesthetics

While creative backgrounds and overlays can enhance a site's aesthetics, it's important to balance this with performance considerations, ensuring that the site loads quickly and runs smoothly.

Accessibility Considerations

Ensure that text remains readable and that interactive elements are distinguishable when using creative backgrounds. Adequate contrast and text shadow can improve readability.

Using Bootstrap Utilities

Leverage Bootstrap's utility classes, such as bg-light or bg-dark, for quick background styling, especially for content or functional elements.

Backgrounds in Bootstrap Cards

Bootstrap cards can be enhanced with backgrounds, either solid colors or images, to make individual cards stand out.

Example with Bootstrap Card

```
<div class="card" style="background-image: url('path/to/image.jpg');">

<div class="card-body">

<h5 class="card-title">Card title</h5>

<p class="card-text">Some quick example text.</p>

</div>

</div>
```

Testing on Various Devices

Always test how backgrounds and overlays render on different devices, especially considering different screen sizes and resolutions.

In conclusion, creative backgrounds and overlays offer a powerful way to enhance the visual appeal and user experience of a website. Whether through stunning imagery, subtle gradients, or dynamic effects, these elements can bring a website's design to life. However, it's important to balance creative expression with considerations for performance, accessibility, and responsive design.

8.3. Advanced Typography Techniques

Effective typography is key to creating engaging and readable web content. Advanced typography techniques involve more than just choosing fonts; they encompass the art of arranging type to make the text visually appealing and easy to read.

Understanding Web Typography

Web typography includes the choice of typeface, size, line length, line-spacing (leading), letter-spacing (tracking), and adjusting the space between pairs of letters (kerning).

Choosing the Right Typeface

Select typefaces that reflect the character of your website and ensure readability. Consider using web-safe fonts or web fonts from services like Google Fonts.

Responsive Typography

Typography should be responsive, adjusting to different screen sizes to ensure readability and a good user experience.

Example of Responsive Typography

body {

font-size: 16px;

line-height: 1.5;

```
}
@media (min-width: 768px) {
body {
font-size: 18px;
}
}
```

This CSS adjusts the font size for larger screens.

Font Pairing

Pairing fonts is an art. Typically, choose one font for your headings and another for your body text. They should complement each other and maintain readability.

Hierarchical Typography

Use different font sizes, weights, and styles to create a clear hierarchy in your content. Headings, subheadings, body text, and captions should be easily distinguishable.

Implementing Hierarchical Typography

```
<h1>Main Heading</h1>
<h2>Subheading</h2>
<p>Body text goes here...</p>
<small>Caption</small>
```

Custom Fonts with @font-face

The @font-face rule allows you to use custom fonts on your website, giving you more control over typography.

Using @font-face

```
@font-face {
font-family: 'MyWebFont';
src: url('webfont.woff2') format('woff2'),
url('webfont.woff') format('woff');
}
```

Then apply it like any other font.

Typography and Mood

Typography can significantly affect the mood of your website. Choose typefaces and styling that align with the tone you want to set.

Text Layout Techniques

Experiment with different text layout techniques like justified text, column layouts, or pull quotes to enhance the visual appeal.

Dynamic Typography with JavaScript

JavaScript can be used to create dynamic typographic effects, such as adjusting font sizes based on screen size or creating interactive typography.

Accessibility in Typography

Ensure that your typography is accessible. This includes sufficient contrast, readable font sizes, and avoiding fonts that are difficult to read.

Web Typography Tools

Tools like Typewolf or Google Fonts can help in choosing and pairing fonts. Adobe Fonts offers a wide range of typefaces for web use.

Typography in Bootstrap

Bootstrap includes typography utilities for text alignment, display headings, lead text, and more. Utilize these tools to quickly implement effective typography.

Example with Bootstrap Typography Utilities

```
<p class="text-center">Center-aligned text.</p>
```

Performance and Web Fonts

Web fonts can impact page load times. Optimize font loading and consider system fonts for better performance.

Advanced CSS Techniques

CSS properties like text-shadow, text-transform, and letter-spacing can be used to add creative touches to your typography.

Experimentation and Testing

Experiment with different typographic styles and layouts. Test your choices with users to see what works best in terms of readability and engagement.

Consistency in Typography

Maintain consistency in your typography throughout your website. This helps in creating a coherent and user-friendly experience.

In conclusion, advanced typography is a crucial element in web design, contributing significantly to the user experience and overall aesthetic of a site. By utilizing responsive design principles, carefully selecting typefaces, and paying attention to details like hierarchy and layout, you can create a visually engaging and accessible website. Bootstrap's typography utilities provide a great foundation, but don't hesitate to explore and experiment beyond these basics to achieve unique and effective typographic designs.

8.4. Implementing Off-canvas Menus

Off-canvas menus have become a popular design pattern in modern web design, particularly for mobile interfaces. They provide an effective way of maximizing screen space while still offering extensive navigation options.

Understanding Off-canvas Menus

An off-canvas menu is typically hidden from view and slides into the screen from the sides (usually from the left or right) upon user interaction, such as a click or a swipe.

The Basics of Off-canvas Design

The off-canvas area is positioned outside of the viewport and is only made visible upon certain user actions. This technique is especially useful for mobile devices where screen real estate is limited.

Implementing Off-canvas Menus in Bootstrap

Bootstrap 5 includes support for off-canvas menus, making it straightforward to implement this functionality.

Basic Off-canvas Menu Example

```
<div class="offcanvas offcanvas-start" id="offcanvasExample" aria-labelledby="offcanvasExampleLabel">

<div class="offcanvas-header">

<h5 class="offcanvas-title" id="offcanvasExampleLabel">Offcanvas</h5>

<button type="button" class="btn-close" data-bs-dismiss="offcanvas" aria-label="Close"></button>

</div>

<div class="offcanvas-body">

<!—Menu items here—>

</div>

</div>
```

This code creates a basic off-canvas menu that slides in from the left.

Styling Off-canvas Menus

Customize the style of your off-canvas menu with CSS to match your website's design. This includes adjusting the width, background color, and typography.

Custom Styling Example

```
.offcanvas {
width: 250px;
background-color: #343a40;
color: white;
}
```

This CSS styles the off-canvas menu with a specific width and color scheme.

Animating Off-canvas Menus

Use CSS transitions to animate the entrance and exit of the off-canvas menu, enhancing the user experience.

CSS Transition Example

```
.offcanvas {
transition: transform 0.3s ease-in-out;
}
```

This provides a smooth transition for the off-canvas menu.

Adding Overlay Effect

An overlay can be added to the main content when the off-canvas menu is open, which helps in focusing user attention on the menu.

Implementing Overlay

```
<div class="offcanvas-backdrop"></div>
```

Use CSS to style the overlay, typically making it semi-transparent.

JavaScript Interactivity

Enhance the functionality of your off-canvas menu with JavaScript. For instance, you can close the menu when a user clicks a menu item or when they click outside the menu.

JavaScript for Closing Menu

```
document.getElementById('close-button').addEventListener('click',
function () {
var offcanvas = document.getElementById('offcanvasExample');
offcanvas.classList.remove('show');
});
```

Accessibility Considerations

Make sure your off-canvas menu is accessible. This includes proper ARIA attributes and ensuring that the menu can be navigated using a keyboard.

Off-canvas Menus for Different Devices

While off-canvas menus are popular for mobile devices, they can also be effective for desktop layouts, particularly for applications or websites with extensive navigation.

Responsive Off-canvas Menus

Ensure that your off-canvas menu adapts to different screen sizes. This might mean changing the menu's position or style on larger screens.

Integrating with Bootstrap's Navbar

Off-canvas menus can be integrated with Bootstrap's navbar component for a cohesive navigation experience.

Navbar with Off-canvas Example

```
<nav class="navbar navbar-expand-lg navbar-light bg-light">

<div class="container-fluid">

<button class="navbar-toggler" type="button" data-bs-toggle="offcanvas" data-bs-target="#offcanvasExample">

<span class="navbar-toggler-icon"></span>

</button>

<!—Rest of navbar content—>

</div>

</nav>
```

This integrates a toggler for the off-canvas menu within the Bootstrap navbar.

Using Off-canvas for More than Menus

Off-canvas areas can be used for more than just menus. Consider using them for shopping carts, search forms, or additional content.

Performance Optimization

Ensure that your off-canvas menu doesn't negatively impact performance, especially on mobile devices. This includes optimizing animations and reducing the complexity of the menu.

Testing and Debugging

Test your off-canvas menu on different devices and browsers to ensure it functions as expected. Pay special attention to touch interactions on mobile devices.

In summary, off-canvas menus are a versatile tool in modern web design, particularly useful for improving user experience on mobile devices. With Bootstrap, implementing an off-canvas menu is streamlined, but it's important to customize and test these menus to ensure they meet the specific needs of your

8.5. Designing for Print

Designing for print involves creating web pages that are not only visually appealing and functional on screen but also when printed. This aspect is often overlooked in web design but is crucial for providing a complete user experience, especially for business or educational websites where users might need to print information.

Understanding the Need for Print-Friendly Design

Not all web content is confined to digital use. Users may need to print articles, reports, receipts, or other information. Ensuring that these printouts are legible and well-formatted is an important aspect of web design.

Key Considerations for Print Design

- Remove unnecessary elements (like navigation menus) in print.
- Ensure text is legible and images are clear in black and white.
- Adjust page layout to fit common print formats.

Using CSS for Print

CSS provides a @media print query that allows you to define specific styles for print. These styles will override the screen styles when the page is printed.

Basic Print CSS Example

```
@media print {
body {
color: black;
background: white;
}
nav, footer {
```

```
display: none;
}
}
```

This CSS hides navigation and footer elements and ensures text is black on a white background when printed.

Typography in Print

Choose fonts and sizes that are legible in print. Remember that decorative fonts might not translate well on paper.

Handling Images in Print

Ensure that images are high-resolution enough to print clearly. Consider replacing or hiding background images that may not be necessary in a print layout.

Print-Specific Layouts

You might need to restructure your layout for print. This could involve simplifying the design, changing the order of elements, or splitting content across pages.

Page Breaks

Control page breaks in print using CSS properties like page-break-before, page-break-after, and page-break-inside to avoid awkward splits in your content.

Implementing Page Breaks

```
@media print {
```

```
h2, h3 {
page-break-before: always;
}
}
```

This ensures that headings start on a new page when printed.

Printable Forms and Tables

Forms and tables often need special attention to ensure they are readable and well-structured when printed.

Testing Print Styles

Regularly test your print styles by actually printing out pages or using print preview in browsers. Ensure that everything aligns correctly and is legible.

Providing a Print Button

Consider adding a print button with JavaScript to offer users an easy way to print the current page.

Print Button Example

```
<button onclick="window.print();">Print this page</button>
```

Avoiding Unnecessary Color

Since many users will print in black and white, design with grayscale printing in mind. Ensure that important elements don't rely solely on color for meaning.

Conserving Ink

Be mindful of ink usage. Avoid large, ink-heavy elements and consider lighter versions of elements for the print version.

Accessibility in Print

Ensure that the printed versions of web pages are accessible, considering users who might have visual impairments or other disabilities.

Incorporating Branding

Maintain your brand identity in the print version, but balance it with the practicalities of print design. This might involve simplified versions of logos and consistent use of brand colors (if color printing is expected).

Documentation and User Guidance

Provide instructions or documentation for users on how to best print pages from your website, if necessary.

Feedback and Iteration

Gather feedback on the usability of your printed web content and be prepared to make iterative improvements based on user needs and experiences.

In conclusion, designing for print is a critical aspect of comprehensive web design. By using CSS media queries for print, paying attention to layout and typography, and considering the practicalities of printed content, you can ensure that your web pages are not only effective on screen but also when printed. This approach enhances the overall usability and user experience of your website.

Chapter 9: Navigational Components

9.1. Building a Responsive Navbar

A responsive navbar is an essential component of modern web design. It acts as the primary navigation tool and should function seamlessly across different devices and screen sizes.

Understanding the Navbar in Bootstrap

Bootstrap's navbar component is designed for responsive behavior. It automatically adjusts for different screen sizes and has support for collapsing and expanding navbar content based on the viewport width.

Basic Structure of a Bootstrap Navbar

```
<nav class="navbar navbar-expand-lg navbar-light bg-light">

<a class="navbar-brand" href="#">Navbar</a>

<button class="navbar-toggler" type="button" data-toggle="collapse" data-target="#navbarNav" aria-controls="navbarNav" aria-expanded="false" aria-label="Toggle navigation">

<span class="navbar-toggler-icon"></span>

</button>

<div class="collapse navbar-collapse" id="navbarNav">

<ul class="navbar-nav">

<li class="nav-item active">
```

```
<a class="nav-link" href="#">Home <span class="sr-only">(current)</span></a>

</li>

<!—More nav items—>

</ul>

</div>

</nav>
```

This is a basic navbar setup in Bootstrap.

Customizing the Navbar

While Bootstrap provides a functional navbar, customizing its style to fit your website's design is crucial. This can involve changing colors, fonts, and layout.

Custom Navbar Styling

```
.navbar-custom {

background-color: #333;

color: #fff;

}
```

Apply the .navbar-custom class to the navbar for custom styling.

Responsive Navbar Collapse

The navbar collapse feature in Bootstrap allows the navbar to be hidden at lower screen sizes and shown via a toggle button.

Implementing a Collapsible Navbar

Use the navbar-expand-* classes to determine the breakpoint at which the navbar should collapse into a hamburger menu.

Dropdowns in Navbars

Dropdown menus can be used within the navbar to organize complex navigation structures in a compact form.

Creating a Dropdown in the Navbar

```
<li class="nav-item dropdown">

<a class="nav-link dropdown-toggle" href="#" id="navbarDropdown" role="button" data-toggle="dropdown" aria-haspopup="true" aria-expanded="false">

Dropdown

</a>

<div class="dropdown-menu" aria-labelledby="navbarDropdown">

<a class="dropdown-item" href="#">Action</a>

<!—More dropdown items—>

</div>

</li>
```

Navbar Accessibility

Ensure your navbar is accessible by providing proper ARIA roles and labels, especially for elements like dropdowns and collapsible menus.

Integrating with Router in SPA

In Single Page Applications (SPAs), integrate the navbar with the routing library (like React Router or Vue Router) to handle navigation.

Example with React Router

```
<NavLink to="/home" className="nav-item nav-link">Home</NavLink>
```

Fixed and Sticky Navbars

Navbars can be fixed to the top or bottom of the viewport or made sticky, staying at the top of the screen as the user scrolls.

Making a Navbar Sticky

```
<nav class="navbar navbar-expand-lg navbar-light bg-light sticky-top">

<!—Navbar content—>

</nav>
```

Handling Large Navigation Structures

For websites with extensive navigation links, consider using mega menus or additional off-canvas menus for better organization.

Mobile-First Design Considerations

Focus on a mobile-first approach, ensuring that the navbar is functional and aesthetically pleasing on smaller screens before scaling up to desktop views.

Optimizing Navbar Performance

Keep the navbar lightweight, avoiding heavy images or complex scripts that can slow down your website, especially important for mobile users.

Testing Across Devices and Browsers

Regularly test the navbar across various devices and browsers to ensure consistent behavior and appearance.

Using Utility Classes

Utilize Bootstrap's utility classes for margin, padding, text alignment, and visibility to fine-tune the navbar's appearance.

Updating Navbar for Branding

Customize the navbar to reflect your brand, using your logo, brand colors, and typography to maintain consistency across your website.

Navbar and SEO

Ensure that navigation links are structured in a way that is friendly for search engines, using clear, descriptive text for links.

User Feedback and Iteration

Gather user feedback on the navbar's usability and make iterative improvements based on real-world usage.

In conclusion, a responsive navbar is a key component of any modern website, serving as the primary means of navigation. By leveraging Bootstrap's navbar component and customizing it to fit the needs of your website, you can create a navigation experience that is both user-friendly and aesthetically pleasing across all devices.

9.2. Dropdowns and Mega Menus

Dropdowns and mega menus are essential components for organizing complex navigation structures in a web design. They allow users to navigate through multiple options without cluttering the primary navigation bar.

Understanding Dropdowns in Bootstrap

Bootstrap provides a straightforward way to create dropdown menus. These menus are hidden elements that are revealed upon user interaction, typically through a hover or click.

Basic Dropdown Implementation

```
<div class="dropdown">

<button class="btn btn-secondary dropdown-toggle" type="button" id="dropdownMenuButton" data-toggle="dropdown" aria-haspopup="true" aria-expanded="false">

Dropdown button

</button>

<div class="dropdown-menu" aria-labelledby="dropdownMenuButton">
```

```
<a class="dropdown-item" href="#">Action</a>

<!—Additional dropdown items—>

</div>

</div>
```

This code creates a basic dropdown button with menu items.

Styling Dropdown Menus

Customize the appearance of dropdown menus to match your site's design. This includes modifying colors, borders, and padding.

Custom Dropdown Styles

```
.dropdown-menu {

background-color: #f8f9fa;

border-color: #ddd;

}
```

Apply custom styles to .dropdown-menu to change the appearance.

Creating Mega Menus

Mega menus are large dropdown menus that can contain multiple columns of links, images, or even forms. They are useful for sites with extensive content.

Structure of a Mega Menu

```
<div class="dropdown-menu mega-menu">
```

```
<div class="row">

<div class="col-md-4">

<!—Column 1 content—>

</div>

<div class="col-md-4">

<!—Column 2 content—>

</div>

<div class="col-md-4">

<!—Column 3 content—>

</div>

</div>

</div>
```

This layout uses Bootstrap's grid system within a dropdown menu to create a mega menu.

Interactivity with JavaScript

Enhance dropdowns and mega menus with JavaScript for additional interactivity, like dynamic content loading or animation effects.

JavaScript for Dropdown Events

```
$('.dropdown').on('show.bs.dropdown', function () {

// Code to execute when a dropdown is shown
```

});

Accessibility in Dropdowns and Mega Menus

Ensure that your dropdowns and mega menus are accessible. This includes proper keyboard navigation and ARIA attributes for screen readers.

Responsive Design for Dropdowns

Adapt your dropdowns for different screen sizes. On mobile devices, consider alternatives to hover-triggered menus.

Hover vs Click Activation

Decide whether dropdowns should open on hover or click. Hover can be convenient for desktop users, but click activation is often more mobile-friendly.

Integrating with the Navbar

Integrate dropdowns and mega menus seamlessly with your site's navbar. They should feel like a natural part of the navigation structure.

Navbar Dropdown Example

```
<li class="nav-item dropdown">

<a class="nav-link dropdown-toggle" href="#" id="navbarDropdown" role="button" data-toggle="dropdown">

Dropdown

</a>
```

<!—Dropdown menu items—>

</li>

Performance Considerations

Keep in mind the performance implications of complex dropdowns and mega menus, especially when including images or dynamic content.

Dropdowns for User Settings

Dropdowns can be effectively used for user settings or account menus in the navbar, keeping these options accessible yet unobtrusive.

Using Icons in Dropdowns

Incorporate icons in your dropdown menus for a more visually appealing and intuitive navigation experience.

Custom Animations and Transitions

Use CSS transitions and animations to add smooth opening and closing effects to dropdowns, enhancing the user experience.

Testing Across Devices and Browsers

Ensure that dropdowns and mega menus work consistently across various devices and browsers, especially given their interactive nature.

User Engagement and Feedback

Monitor how users interact with your dropdowns and mega menus. User feedback can be invaluable in refining their design and functionality.

In summary, dropdowns and mega menus are versatile tools for handling complex navigation structures in web design. With Bootstrap, creating and customizing these components is straightforward. However, it's important to consider aspects such as accessibility, responsiveness, and user experience to ensure that they enhance the overall navigation of your website.

9.3. Breadcrumbs and Pagination

Breadcrumbs and pagination are crucial navigational components, especially for websites with a lot of content, such as e-commerce sites, blogs, and informational sites. They help users understand their location within the site and navigate through pages efficiently.

Understanding Breadcrumbs

Breadcrumbs are a type of secondary navigation scheme that reveal the user's location in a website or application. They are especially useful for sites with multiple levels of content hierarchy.

Implementing Breadcrumbs in Bootstrap

Bootstrap provides a simple way to add breadcrumbs to your site.

```
<nav aria-label="breadcrumb">

<ol class="breadcrumb">

<li class="breadcrumb-item"><a href="#">Home</a></li>
```

```
<li class="breadcrumb-item"><a href="#">Library</a></li>

<li class="breadcrumb-item active" aria-current="page">Data</li>

</ol>

</nav>
```

This markup creates a basic breadcrumb trail.

Styling Breadcrumbs

While Bootstrap offers a default style for breadcrumbs, customizing them to match your site's design enhances the overall look and feel.

Custom Breadcrumb Styles

```
.breadcrumb {

background-color: #f8f9fa;

color: #0275d8;

}
```

Customize the background color and text color of breadcrumbs.

Pagination Basics

Pagination is the process of dividing web content into discrete pages, which is essential for improving the usability of sites with large amounts of content.

Basic Pagination in Bootstrap

Bootstrap's pagination component is easy to implement.

```
<nav aria-label="Page navigation example">

<ul class="pagination">

<li class="page-item"><a class="page-link" href="#">Previous</a></li>

<!—Pagination items—>

<li class="page-item"><a class="page-link" href="#">Next</a></li>

</ul>

</nav>
```

This creates a simple pagination bar.

Customizing Pagination

Adapt the style of pagination to fit the design of your site. This can include changing sizes, colors, and borders.

Styling Pagination

```
.pagination .page-link {

color: #0275d8;

background-color: #fff;

border: 1px solid #ddd;

}
```

Custom styles for pagination links.

Dynamic Breadcrumbs

For dynamic sites, especially those with a complex structure, generate breadcrumbs programmatically based on the user's navigation path.

Accessible Breadcrumbs and Pagination

Ensure that breadcrumbs and pagination components are accessible, with appropriate ARIA labels and roles.

Pagination with Large Number of Pages

For sites with a large number of pages, consider using condensed pagination, showing only the first, last, and nearby pages to the current page.

Condensed Pagination Example

```
<ul class="pagination">

<li class="page-item"><a class="page-link" href="#">1</a></li>

<li class="page-item disabled"><span class="page-link">...</span></li>

<!—Nearby pages—>

<li class="page-item disabled"><span class="page-link">...</span></li>

<li class="page-item"><a class="page-link" href="#">Last</a></li>

</ul>
```

Breadcrumbs for SEO

Breadcrumbs can also have SEO benefits by providing a clear hierarchy, which can be understood by search engines.

Integrating Pagination with Content

Ensure that your pagination is well-integrated with the content, offering a seamless user experience when navigating through pages.

Responsive Design

Both breadcrumbs and pagination should be responsive, adapting to different screen sizes without losing functionality.

Pagination in Single Page Applications (SPA)

In SPAs, handle pagination with care, ensuring that it integrates well with the JavaScript framework or library used.

Testing User Navigation

Regularly test how users interact with your breadcrumbs and pagination to identify any usability issues.

Keeping Breadcrumbs Up-to-Date

In dynamic sites, ensure that breadcrumbs are updated in real-time as users navigate through the site.

Visual Hierarchy in Breadcrumbs

Maintain a clear visual hierarchy in breadcrumbs, distinguishing between different levels and the current page.

In conclusion, breadcrumbs and pagination are key navigational components that enhance the usability of websites with extensive content. They provide users with a clear understanding of their location within the site and a convenient way to navigate through pages. With Bootstrap, implementing these components is straightforward, but they should be customized and tested to ensure they meet the specific needs of your audience and align with the design and functionality of your site.

9.4. Vertical Navigation and Sidebars

Vertical navigation and sidebars are essential elements in many web designs, offering an efficient way to present additional navigational links, tools, or information in a compact and organized manner.

Understanding Vertical Navigation

Vertical navigation refers to a menu or set of links displayed vertically, typically on the side of a page. This layout is particularly useful for dashboards, admin panels, and websites with extensive navigation.

Basic Vertical Navigation Structure

```
<div class="vertical-nav">

<ul>

<li><a href="#">Home</a></li>

<li><a href="#">Services</a></li>

<li><a href="#">About</a></li>

<!—More links—>
```

```
</ul>

</div>
```

This markup creates a basic vertical navigation menu.

Designing Sidebars

A sidebar is a vertical navigation panel that often contains additional content like contact information, search bars, or call-to-action buttons, alongside navigation links.

Sidebar Implementation Example

```
<aside class="sidebar">

<nav>

<!—Navigation links—>

</nav>

<div>

<!—Additional sidebar content—>

</div>

</aside>
```

Styling Vertical Navigation and Sidebars

Customize the style of your vertical navigation and sidebars to match your website's overall design. This includes adjusting widths, colors, and typography.

Custom Styles for Vertical Navigation

```
.vertical-nav {
width: 200px;
background-color: #f8f9fa;
/* Additional styles */
}
```

Responsive Design Considerations

Ensure that your vertical navigation and sidebars are responsive. On smaller screens, they can be transformed into collapsible menus or off-canvas elements.

Integrating with Bootstrap Grid

Use Bootstrap's grid system to integrate vertical navigation or sidebars into your layout seamlessly.

Example with Bootstrap Grid

```
<div class="container-fluid">
<div class="row">
<div class="col-md-3">
<!—Sidebar content—>
</div>
<div class="col-md-9">
```

```
<!—Main content—>

</div>

</div>

</div>
```

Accessibility in Vertical Navigation

Make your vertical navigation accessible with proper semantic HTML, ARIA roles, and keyboard navigation.

Using Icons in Vertical Navigation

Icons can enhance the usability and visual appeal of vertical navigation menus. Choose icons that are intuitive and match the link's purpose.

Example with Icons

```
<ul class="vertical-nav">

<li><a href="#"><i class="fas fa-home"></i> Home</a></li>

<!—More links with icons—>

</ul>
```

Hover and Active States

Define clear hover and active states for links in your vertical navigation to improve user experience and orientation.

Nested Menus in Vertical Navigation

For complex navigation structures, consider using nested menus that can expand and collapse within the vertical navigation.

Nested Menu Example

```
<ul class="vertical-nav">

<li>

<a href="#submenu1" data-toggle="collapse">Services</a>

<ul class="collapse" id="submenu1">

<li><a href="#">Web Design</a></li>

<!—More nested items—>

</ul>

</li>

<!—More items—>

</ul>
```

Sticky Sidebars

A sticky sidebar remains fixed on the screen as the user scrolls, making it constantly accessible.

CSS for Sticky Sidebar

```
.sidebar {

position: sticky;
```

top: 0;

}

Collapsible Sidebars for Mobile

On mobile devices, space is limited, so consider making sidebars collapsible or converting them into a dropdown menu.

Sidebars for Additional Content

Sidebars can be used not only for navigation but also to display additional content like calendars, advertisements, or profile information.

Performance Optimization

Optimize the performance of your vertical navigation and sidebars, particularly if they contain images, dynamic content, or complex scripts.

User Interaction and Feedback

Observe how users interact with your vertical navigation or sidebar. User feedback can guide iterative improvements to enhance usability and effectiveness.

Testing Across Devices and Browsers

Regularly test your vertical navigation and sidebars across different devices and browsers to ensure consistent performance and appearance.

In conclusion, vertical navigation and sidebars are versatile components that can significantly enhance the functionality and aesthetics of a website. With careful design, customization, and responsiveness in mind, they can provide an effective and user-friendly means of navigating and presenting additional content on your site.

9.5. Scrollspy for Dynamic Navigation

Scrollspy is a feature in Bootstrap that automatically updates navigation links based on scroll position, highlighting which section of the page is currently in the viewport. It's particularly useful for single-page websites or long pages with several sections.

Understanding Scrollspy in Bootstrap

Bootstrap's Scrollspy listens to the page scroll events and automatically updates the navigation links' active state based on the scroll position.

Basic Scrollspy Setup

```
<body data-bs-spy="scroll" data-bs-target="#navbar-example">

<div id="navbar-example">

<ul class="nav nav-tabs">

<li class="nav-item"><a class="nav-link" href="#section1">Section 1</a></li>

<!—More nav links—>

</ul>

</div>

<section id="section1">...</section>
```

<!—More sections—>

</body>

This code attaches Scrollspy to the body, targeting the navigation bar with the id navbar-example.

Implementing Dynamic Navigation

Dynamic navigation becomes more interactive with Scrollspy, as it reflects the user's current reading position in the document.

Customizing Scrollspy Behavior

You can customize Scrollspy by adjusting its offset, which is the number of pixels before the scroll position that the navigation item becomes active.

Adjusting Scrollspy Offset

<body data-bs-spy="scroll" **data-bs-target=**"#navbar-example" **data-bs-offset=**"100"**>**

<!—Content—>

</body>

An offset of 100px means the nav link becomes active when the corresponding section is 100px from the top of the viewport.

Responsive Design with Scrollspy

Ensure that your Scrollspy-enhanced navigation is responsive, working seamlessly across various device sizes.

Styling Active States

Customize the appearance of active states in your navigation to make them stand out. This can involve changing colors, borders, or font sizes.

Active State Styling

```
.nav-link.active {
font-weight: bold;
color: #007bff;
}
```

This styles the active navigation link with a bolder font and a different color.

Smooth Scrolling

Enhance the user experience by implementing smooth scrolling when navigation links are clicked. This can be done using CSS or JavaScript.

CSS for Smooth Scrolling

```
html {
scroll-behavior: smooth;
}
```

This enables smooth scrolling for the entire document.

Integrating with Complex Layouts

Scrollspy can be integrated into complex layouts, such as those with fixed headers or multiple columns, with some additional considerations for offsets and positioning.

Nested Navigation with Scrollspy

For nested navigation structures, ensure that Scrollspy correctly updates the active state of both parent and child navigation items.

Updating Scrollspy with Dynamic Content

If your page's content changes dynamically (e.g., loading content via AJAX), update Scrollspy to recognize these changes.

Refreshing Scrollspy

```
var dataSpyList = [].slice.call(document.querySelectorAll('[data-bs-spy="scroll"]'))

dataSpyList.forEach(function (dataSpyEl) {

bootstrap.ScrollSpy.getInstance(dataSpyEl).refresh()

})
```

Accessibility Considerations

Ensure that your navigation is accessible, with proper ARIA roles and keyboard navigation compatibility, even with Scrollspy implemented.

Performance Optimization

Optimize performance, especially if your page is long or complex. Debounce scroll events or use requestAnimationFrame for better performance.

Testing Across Browsers and Devices

Test your implementation across different browsers and devices to ensure consistent behavior, especially where smooth scrolling and fixed elements are involved.

User Feedback and Iteration

Monitor how users interact with your navigation. User feedback can be invaluable in refining Scrollspy's implementation and settings.

Documentation and Guidelines

Provide clear documentation or guidelines on how to navigate your site using the dynamic navigation enhanced by Scrollspy.

In conclusion, Scrollspy is a powerful tool in Bootstrap that adds a dynamic and interactive element to page navigation. By highlighting the active section in the viewport, it greatly enhances the user experience on long or single-page websites. Proper implementation, customization, and testing are key to ensuring that it functions effectively across all devices and browsers.

Chapter 10: Extending Bootstrap

10.1. Integrating Third-party Libraries

Integrating third-party libraries with Bootstrap can greatly enhance the functionality and aesthetic appeal of web projects. This practice allows developers to tap into a vast ecosystem of tools and plugins that complement Bootstrap's capabilities.

Understanding Third-party Library Integration

Third-party libraries are external JavaScript or CSS files that add additional functionalities or styles to a website. These can range from complex UI components to utility libraries.

Examples of Popular Libraries

- jQuery UI: A collection of GUI widgets, animated visual effects, and themes.

- Chart.js: A simple yet flexible JavaScript charting library.

- Animate.css: A library for CSS animations.

Assessing Compatibility

Before integrating a third-party library, assess its compatibility with Bootstrap, especially considering Bootstrap's own JavaScript components and CSS styles.

Managing Dependencies

Use package managers like npm or Yarn to manage third-party library dependencies, ensuring easy updates and compatibility checks.

Example: Installing a Package via npm

```
npm install chart.js
```

Integrating JavaScript Libraries

To integrate a JavaScript library, include its script file in your HTML. Ensure it does not conflict with Bootstrap's JavaScript.

Example: Including Chart.js

```
<script src="path/to/chartjs/dist/chart.js"></script>
```

Integrating CSS Libraries

Similarly, integrate CSS libraries by including their stylesheet files. Ensure that the library's styles don't conflict with Bootstrap's CSS.

Example: Including Animate.css

```
<link rel="stylesheet" href="path/to/animate.css/animate.min.css">
```

Customizing Library Components

Many third-party libraries offer customization options. Tailor these components to fit the design and functionality of your Bootstrap project.

Handling Library Updates

Stay updated with changes and updates to the libraries you use. Keep an eye on compatibility changes, especially when updating Bootstrap or the library itself.

Enhancing UI Components

Use libraries to enhance Bootstrap's UI components, like adding advanced features to modals, tabs, or accordions.

Performance Considerations

Be mindful of the performance impact of adding third-party libraries. Evaluate the library's size and potential impact on load times.

Avoiding Conflicts

Be aware of potential conflicts between Bootstrap's JavaScript and that of third-party libraries. For instance, jQuery UI and Bootstrap can conflict due to overlapping widget names.

Responsive Design

Ensure that the integrated libraries work well in a responsive context and do not break Bootstrap's responsive features.

Accessibility Compliance

Check if the third-party library components are accessible and meet WCAG standards, especially for UI components like sliders, date pickers, or dialogs.

Testing Across Environments

Test your website across different browsers and devices to ensure that the integrated libraries function consistently alongside Bootstrap.

Documentation and Community Support

Explore the documentation and community support available for the third-party library. This can be invaluable for troubleshooting and best practices.

Integrating with Build Tools

Incorporate library integration into your build process using tools like Webpack or Gulp, especially for larger projects.

Custom Builds

Some libraries offer custom builds where you can select only the components you need, helping to reduce the overall size.

Legal and Licensing Considerations

Check the licensing of the third-party library to ensure it's compatible with your project's requirements and that you're complying with its terms of use.

Keeping Up with Updates

Regularly monitor updates for both Bootstrap and the third-party libraries to take advantage of new features and security updates.

In conclusion, integrating third-party libraries with Bootstrap can significantly extend the capabilities of your web projects. It's important to carefully select and integrate these libraries, keeping in mind factors such as compatibility, performance, and maintainability. Proper integration can result in a more powerful, feature-rich, and visually appealing web application.

10.2. Bootstrap Plugins and Extensions

Bootstrap, being a versatile framework, can be extended with various plugins and extensions to enhance its functionality and user experience. These plugins and extensions can range from simple UI enhancements to complex interactive components.

Exploring Bootstrap Plugins

Plugins are additional JavaScript components that extend the functionality of Bootstrap. They can add new features or enhance existing ones.

Examples of Bootstrap Plugins

- Lightbox for Bootstrap: A plugin to create a lightbox effect for images and galleries.
- Bootstrap Select: Enhances the standard Bootstrap dropdown with additional features.

Choosing the Right Plugins

When selecting plugins, consider factors like compatibility with your Bootstrap version, the plugin's performance, and its community support.

Implementing a Bootstrap Plugin

Integrating a plugin typically involves including its JavaScript and CSS files in your project, and then initializing the plugin in your HTML.

Example: Integrating Bootstrap Select

```
<!—Include Bootstrap Select CSS and JS after Bootstrap's files—>

<link rel="stylesheet" href="bootstrap-select/css/bootstrap-select.min.css">

<script src="bootstrap-select/js/bootstrap-select.min.js"></script>

<!—Usage in HTML—>

<select class="selectpicker">

<option>Option 1</option>

<!—More options—>

</select>
```

Customizing Plugins

Many plugins offer customization options, either through data attributes in HTML or via JavaScript. Customize them to fit the design and functionality of your website.

Creating Your Own Bootstrap Plugins

If existing plugins don't meet your needs, you can create your own. Bootstrap's JavaScript API provides a solid foundation for developing custom plugins.

Basic Structure of a Custom Plugin

```
(function($) {
$.fn.myCustomPlugin = function(options) {
// Plugin logic here
};
})(jQuery);
```

This is a template for a jQuery-based Bootstrap plugin.

Ensuring Responsive Behavior

Make sure that any plugins used or created are responsive and don't break Bootstrap's responsive layout.

Accessibility Considerations

Your plugins should be accessible, following best practices such as keyboard navigability and ARIA roles.

Performance Optimization

Be mindful of the performance impact of adding plugins. Optimize JavaScript and CSS, and only load plugins when necessary.

Handling Conflicts

Avoid conflicts with Bootstrap's core JavaScript and other plugins. Namespace your custom plugins and test for compatibility.

Updating and Maintenance

Regularly update your plugins to stay compatible with new Bootstrap versions. If you've created a custom plugin, maintain it by fixing bugs and adding features.

Documentation and Usage Guidelines

If you develop a custom plugin, provide clear documentation and usage guidelines for other developers.

Security Aspects

Ensure that your plugins are secure and don't expose vulnerabilities, particularly if they handle user data or interact with backend systems.

Testing Across Browsers and Devices

Test the plugins across various browsers and devices to ensure consistent behavior and appearance.

Integrating with Build Processes

Incorporate plugin integration into your build process, especially if you are using tools like Webpack or Gulp.

Contributing to the Community

If you create a custom Bootstrap plugin that could be beneficial to others, consider open-sourcing it and contributing to the Bootstrap community.

Learning from Existing Plugins

Study existing popular Bootstrap plugins to understand best practices in plugin development and Bootstrap integration.

In conclusion, Bootstrap plugins and extensions are powerful tools for enhancing the capabilities of Bootstrap-based projects. Whether using existing plugins or creating custom ones, it's crucial to ensure they are compatible, responsive, accessible, and maintainable. Proper integration and customization of plugins can lead to a richer, more interactive, and user-friendly web experience.

10.3. Custom JavaScript Additions

Custom JavaScript additions can greatly enhance the functionality of Bootstrap-based websites, allowing developers to tailor the user experience to specific requirements. These custom scripts can range from simple modifications to complex, interactive features.

Understanding Custom JavaScript with Bootstrap

While Bootstrap provides a range of interactive components, sometimes specific project needs require custom JavaScript. This could be for new features or to modify existing Bootstrap components.

Example: Custom Toggle Button

```
document.querySelector('.custom-toggle').addEventListener('click', function() {

document.querySelector('.target-element').classList.toggle('active');

});
```

This script toggles a class on an element, demonstrating a simple interaction.

Enhancing Bootstrap Components

Use custom JavaScript to enhance or extend the functionality of Bootstrap components, such as adding new behaviors to modals or dropdowns.

Enhancing a Modal

```
$('#myModal').on('shown.bs.modal', function () {

// Custom actions to perform when the modal is shown

});
```

Integrating with Third-party APIs

Custom JavaScript can be used to integrate third-party APIs, such as fetching data from a server and displaying it in a Bootstrap component.

API Integration Example

```
fetch('https://api.example.com/data')

.then(response => response.json())

.then(data => {

document.querySelector('#api-data').textContent =
JSON.stringify(data);

});
```

Creating Interactive Elements

Build interactive user interface elements that respond to user actions, enhancing the interactivity of your website.

Form Validation and Processing

Improve form handling with custom JavaScript, providing real-time validation feedback or processing form data without a page reload.

Custom Form Validation

```
document.querySelector('#myForm').addEventListener('submit',
function(event) {

if (!this.checkValidity()) {

event.preventDefault();

event.stopPropagation();

}

this.classList.add('was-validated');

});
```

Custom Animations and Transitions

Use JavaScript to create custom animations and transitions for elements, providing a more dynamic user experience.

Animation with JavaScript

```
document.querySelector('.animate-btn').addEventListener('click',
function() {
```

```
document.querySelector('.animated-element').animate([
// keyframes
{ transform: 'translateX(0px)' },
{ transform: 'translateX(100px)' }
], {
// timing options
duration: 1000,
iterations: 1
});
});
```

Event Handling and Delegation

Manage events more efficiently using event delegation, especially for dynamically generated content.

Event Delegation

```
document.querySelector('.parent-element').addEventListener('click', function(event) {
if (event.target.matches('.child-element')) {
// Handle click
}
});
```

Optimizing for Performance

Ensure your custom JavaScript is optimized for performance, avoiding large scripts or inefficient operations that could slow down your website.

Responsive JavaScript

Make sure that your JavaScript functions well in a responsive context, adapting to different device sizes and capabilities.

Error Handling and Debugging

Implement robust error handling in your scripts and test them thoroughly to prevent unexpected behavior or crashes.

Leveraging JavaScript Libraries

Incorporate external JavaScript libraries for specific functionalities, like charting or animations, to enhance your Bootstrap project.

Keeping JavaScript Unobtrusive

Write JavaScript that enhances the user experience without being intrusive. Avoid excessive reliance on JavaScript for essential website functionalities.

Browser Compatibility

Test your custom JavaScript across different browsers to ensure compatibility, especially with older browsers.

Accessibility Considerations

Ensure that any JavaScript-driven features are accessible, providing keyboard navigation and ARIA roles where necessary.

Modular JavaScript

Write modular JavaScript, breaking down functionalities into reusable functions or components, which can simplify maintenance and updates.

Documentation and Comments

Document your JavaScript code thoroughly, providing clear comments and usage instructions, which is especially important for larger projects or teams.

Regular Updates and Refactoring

Regularly review and update your JavaScript code to refactor as necessary, improve performance, and adapt to new web standards.

In conclusion, custom JavaScript additions are a powerful way to enhance and personalize Bootstrap-based projects. Whether it's for adding new functionalities, integrating third-party services, or improving user interaction, custom JavaScript, when used effectively, can significantly elevate the capabilities and user experience of a web application.

10.4. Advanced SASS and CSS Tricks

Advanced SASS and CSS tricks can significantly enhance the styling capabilities of a Bootstrap project, allowing for more sophisticated designs and efficient code management. SASS (Syntactically Awesome Style Sheets) extends CSS with features like variables, nested rules, and mixins, making your stylesheets more powerful and easier to maintain.

Leveraging SASS in Bootstrap

Bootstrap is built with SASS, which means you can use its variables, mixins, and functions to customize your styles effectively.

Using Bootstrap Variables

```
$theme-colors: (
"primary": #007bff,
"success": #28a745,
"info": #17a2b8
);
// Import Bootstrap's source files
@import "node_modules/bootstrap/scss/bootstrap";
```

This customizes the theme colors before importing Bootstrap's SASS files.

Creating Custom Mixins

Mixins in SASS are reusable blocks of code. Create your own mixins to handle repetitive styling patterns efficiently.

Example of a Custom Mixin

```
@mixin flex-center {
display: flex;
justify-content: center;
```

```
align-items: center;
}
.my-div {
@include flex-center;
}
```

Nested SASS Rules

Nesting allows you to structure your CSS in a way that mirrors your HTML, making it more readable and maintainable.

Nested Rules Example

```
.navbar {
.nav-item {
.nav-link {
color: #fff;
&:hover {
color: #ccc;
}
}
}
}
```

Extending Bootstrap Classes with SASS

Extend Bootstrap classes in SASS to create new classes that inherit properties from Bootstrap classes.

Extending a Bootstrap Class

```
.my-custom-btn {

@extend .btn;

background-color: #007bff;

}
```

Using SASS Functions

SASS functions allow you to perform complex operations and calculations within your stylesheets.

Example of a SASS Function

```
@function calculate-rem($size) {

$base-font-size: 16px; // Default browser font size

@return ($size / $base-font-size) * 1rem;

}

p {

font-size: calculate-rem(18px);

}
```

Advanced CSS Selectors

Utilize advanced CSS selectors like child, adjacent sibling, and attribute selectors to target specific elements in more complex ways.

Advanced Selector Example

```
div[class^="col-"] {
padding: 15px;
}
```

This targets all div elements whose class starts with col-.

Responsive Typography

Implement responsive typography using CSS and SASS. Adjust font sizes, line heights, and weights based on the viewport size.

Responsive Typography with SASS

```
h1 {
font-size: 2rem;
@media (min-width: 768px) {
font-size: 2.5rem;
}
}
```

Animation with SASS

Create animations and transitions with SASS for more interactive user interfaces.

Animation Example

```
@keyframes fadeIn {
from { opacity: 0; }
to { opacity: 1; }
}
.fade-in {
animation: fadeIn 1s ease-in-out;
}
```

Organizing SASS Files

For larger projects, organize your SASS files into partials and modules, and import them into a main stylesheet. This improves scalability and maintainability.

Theming with SASS

Use SASS to create themes for your site by defining different sets of variables and styles that can be switched dynamically.

CSS Grid and Flexbox

Combine Bootstrap's grid system with CSS Grid and Flexbox for more complex layouts and alignment.

Custom Media Queries

Write custom media queries to handle responsive styling for specific components or layouts that aren't covered by Bootstrap's breakpoints.

Custom Media Query

```
.my-component {
@media (max-width: 600px) {
// Styles for mobile devices
}
}
```

Optimizing CSS Output

When compiling SASS, use tools like PostCSS to optimize the output, including minification and autoprefixing.

Browser Testing and Compatibility

Regularly test your SASS and CSS across different browsers to ensure compatibility, especially when using advanced features.

In conclusion, mastering advanced SASS and CSS techniques can significantly elevate the design and functionality of your Bootstrap projects. By leveraging the power of SASS and combining it with sophisticated CSS practices, you can create more dynamic, efficient, and visually appealing web applications.

10.5. Community Resources and Support

Bootstrap's widespread popularity means there is a vast community of developers and a wealth of resources available. These resources range from forums and discussion boards to template repositories and customization tools, all of which can support and enhance your work with Bootstrap.

Leveraging Online Communities

Online communities are invaluable for getting support, sharing knowledge, and staying updated with the latest trends and best practices in Bootstrap.

Popular Bootstrap Communities

- Stack Overflow: A vast community for asking questions and getting answers.
- Reddit: Subreddits like r/bootstrap are active with discussions and tips.
- Official Bootstrap Slack and Discord channels.

Bootstrap Templates and Themes

There are numerous sites offering Bootstrap templates and themes, both free and paid, which can serve as a starting point for your projects or provide inspiration.

Finding Bootstrap Templates

- ThemeForest: A marketplace for premium Bootstrap templates.

- Start Bootstrap: Offers free, open-source templates for various types of projects.

Customization Tools

Tools like Bootstrap Studio or Pinegrow offer graphical interfaces for designing and customizing Bootstrap websites, making the process more accessible to those less familiar with coding.

Using Bootstrap Builders

- Bootstrap Studio: A powerful desktop app for designing and prototyping websites.

- Pinegrow: A desktop web editor that lets you build responsive websites faster with live multi-page editing.

Extending Bootstrap with Add-ons

Numerous add-ons and plugins can be integrated with Bootstrap to extend its functionality, from advanced form validators to complex UI components.

Bootstrap Cheat Sheets

Cheat sheets are handy references for Bootstrap classes and components, saving time and enhancing productivity.

Bootstrap Cheat Sheet Example

- BootstrapCreative: Offers a comprehensive cheat sheet for Bootstrap classes and components.

Video Tutorials and Online Courses

There are many video tutorials and online courses available that cover various aspects of Bootstrap, suitable for beginners and advanced users alike.

Bootstrap Learning Resources

- Udemy: Hosts a range of courses on Bootstrap for all levels.
- YouTube: Channels like Traversy Media provide free tutorials and guides.

Forums for Problem-Solving

Participate in forums dedicated to web development and Bootstrap. These can be great places to ask specific questions and get targeted advice.

Blogs and Articles

Follow blogs and articles that focus on Bootstrap and front-end development. They can provide valuable insights, tips, and updates.

Bootstrap-Focused Blogs

- Official Bootstrap Blog: Provides updates, release notes, and tips.
- Smashing Magazine: Publishes articles on web development including Bootstrap.

GitHub Repositories

Explore GitHub for open-source Bootstrap projects and contributions. It's also a place to report issues and contribute to the Bootstrap codebase.

Bootstrap Events and Meetups

Attend Bootstrap-themed events, conferences, and meetups to network with other developers and learn from their experiences.

Books and eBooks

Several comprehensive books and eBooks are available that cover Bootstrap in-depth, suitable for those who prefer structured learning.

Keeping Up with Bootstrap Updates

Stay informed about updates and new releases of Bootstrap. Following the official Bootstrap blog or Twitter account can be helpful.

Contributing to the Bootstrap Community

If you have gained expertise in Bootstrap, consider giving back to the community by answering questions, contributing to open source projects, or writing blogs and tutorials.

In conclusion, the Bootstrap community is a rich resource for developers of all levels. By engaging with these resources, you can enhance your skills, solve complex problems, and stay updated with the latest advancements in Bootstrap. Whether you are a beginner or an experienced developer, the community has something to offer everyone.

Chapter 11: Bootstrap and eCommerce

11.1 Designing eCommerce Websites with Bootstrap

In this section, we'll explore how to leverage Bootstrap to design effective eCommerce websites. E-commerce sites require careful planning and design to ensure a seamless shopping experience for users. Bootstrap provides a solid foundation for creating responsive and visually appealing online stores. Let's dive into the key aspects of designing eCommerce websites using Bootstrap.

11.1.1 Planning Your eCommerce Site

Before you start designing your eCommerce site with Bootstrap, it's essential to have a clear plan. Consider the following:

Define Your Product Categories

Determine the categories of products you'll be selling. Organize them logically to help users navigate your site easily.

User Flow and Navigation

Map out the user journey from landing on your site to making a purchase. Plan the navigation structure, including menus, search functionality, and filters.

11.1.2 Setting Up the Product Listings

Bootstrap's grid system is invaluable for creating product listings. You can use the grid to display products in a clean and organized manner. Here's a basic example:

```
<div class="row">

<div class="col-md-4">

<!—Product 1—>

</div>

<div class="col-md-4">

<!—Product 2—>

</div>

<div class="col-md-4">

<!—Product 3—>

</div>

</div>
```

11.1.3 Implementing Filters and Sorting

Allow users to filter products by category, price, brand, and other relevant attributes. Bootstrap's form components and JavaScript plugins can help you create interactive filters.

```
<form>

<div class="form-group">

<label for="category">Category:</label>

<select class="form-control" id="category">

<option>Category 1</option>

<option>Category 2</option>
```

```
<!—Add more categories—>

</select>

</div>

</form>
```

11.1.4 Shopping Cart and Checkout Pages

Designing the shopping cart and checkout pages is crucial. Bootstrap offers components like modals and forms to create a seamless checkout process.

```
<!—Shopping Cart Modal—>

<div class="modal fade" id="cartModal" tabindex="-1" role="dialog" aria-labelledby="cartModalLabel" aria-hidden="true">

<!—Modal content—>

</div>
```

11.1.5 Responsive Product Galleries

Ensure that product images and galleries are responsive. Bootstrap's image classes and responsive utilities can help you achieve this.

```
<img src="product-image.jpg" class="img-fluid" alt="Product Image">
```

11.1.6 Payment Forms and Security

When it comes to handling payments, ensure the use of secure and compliant payment gateways. Bootstrap can help you style payment forms and ensure a secure transaction process.

```
<form>

<div class="form-group">

<label for="creditCard">Credit Card Number:</label>

<input type="text" class="form-control" id="creditCard" placeholder="Enter your card number">

</div>

</form>
```

Remember that eCommerce sites also need proper security measures and compliance with data protection regulations.

Designing an eCommerce website with Bootstrap requires attention to detail and a user-centric approach. By following best practices and utilizing Bootstrap's components and features, you can create a visually appealing and functional online store that enhances the shopping experience for your customers.

Now, let's move on to the next section, where we'll explore product listings and filters in more detail.

11.2 Product Listings and Filters

In this section, we will delve deeper into creating effective product listings and implementing filters for your Bootstrap-powered eCommerce website. A well-organized product listing and intuitive filtering system are essential components to enhance user experience and drive sales.

11.2.1 Structuring Product Listings

Product listings are the heart of any eCommerce site. Bootstrap's grid system is a valuable tool for structuring product listings in a visually pleasing and responsive way. You can use various grid classes to display product details such as name, price, and image.

```
<div class="row">

<div class="col-lg-3 col-md-4 col-sm-6">

<div class="product">

<img src="product1.jpg" alt="Product 1">

<h4>Product Name</h4>

<p>$49.99</p>

<button class="btn btn-primary">Add to Cart</button>

</div>

</div>

<!—Add more product items—>

</div>
```

Make sure to customize the grid classes based on the number of products you want to display per row and the device screen size.

11.2.2 Sorting and Filtering Options

Allow users to sort and filter products based on their preferences. Bootstrap can assist in creating interactive filters and sorting options. Here's an example of a simple filter bar using Bootstrap's dropdown component:

```
<div class="dropdown">

<button class="btn btn-secondary dropdown-toggle" type="button" id="filterDropdown" data-toggle="dropdown" aria-haspopup="true" aria-expanded="false">

Filter by Category

</button>

<div class="dropdown-menu" aria-labelledby="filterDropdown">

<a class="dropdown-item" href="#">Category 1</a>

<a class="dropdown-item" href="#">Category 2</a>

<!—Add more categories—>

</div>

</div>
```

You can also add sorting options for price, popularity, and other relevant attributes.

11.2.3 Product Detail Pages

When a user clicks on a product, it's essential to provide them with a detailed product page. Bootstrap's components, such as modals or dedicated product detail pages, can be used to display comprehensive product information, images, and user reviews.

```
<!—Product Detail Modal—>

<div class="modal fade" id="productDetailModal" tabindex="-1" role="dialog" aria-labelledby="productDetailModalLabel" aria-hidden="true">
```

```
<!—Modal content—>

</div>
```

11.2.4 Pagination for Large Inventories

For eCommerce sites with a large inventory, consider implementing pagination to break down product listings into manageable sections. Bootstrap offers pagination components that can be integrated easily.

```
<ul class="pagination">

<li class="page-item"><a class="page-link" href="#">1</a></li>

<li class="page-item"><a class="page-link" href="#">2</a></li>

<!—Add more pages as needed—>

</ul>
```

11.2.5 Mobile-Friendly Product Listings

Remember to ensure that your product listings are mobile-friendly. Bootstrap's responsive classes and utilities help in adapting product listings for various screen sizes.

```
<div class="row">

<div class="col-md-4 col-6">

<!—Product Item—>

</div>

<!—Add more product items—>

</div>
```

By structuring product listings effectively, providing sorting and filtering options, and ensuring mobile responsiveness, you can create a user-friendly and visually appealing product browsing experience on your Bootstrap-powered eCommerce website. Next, we'll explore shopping cart and checkout pages in detail in the upcoming section.

11.3 Shopping Cart and Checkout Pages

In this section, we'll focus on designing shopping cart and checkout pages for your Bootstrap-based eCommerce website. These pages are critical for converting visitors into customers and ensuring a smooth purchasing process.

11.3.1 Shopping Cart Page

The shopping cart page is where users can review the items they've added before proceeding to checkout. Bootstrap offers components to create a well-structured cart page.

```
<div class="container">

<div class="row">

<div class="col-md-8">

<!—Cart Items—>

<div class="cart-item">

<img src="product.jpg" alt="Product Image">

<div class="item-details">

<h4>Product Name</h4>

<p>Price: $49.99</p>
```

```
<p>Quantity: 2</p>
<button class="btn btn-danger">Remove</button>
</div>
</div>
<!—Add more cart items—>
</div>
<div class="col-md-4">
<!—Cart Summary—>
<div class="cart-summary">
<h5>Cart Total</h5>
<p>Subtotal: $99.98</p>
<p>Shipping: $5.00</p>
<h4>Total: $104.98</h4>
<button class="btn btn-success">Proceed to Checkout</button>
</div>
</div>
</div>
</div>
```

Ensure that the cart page provides clear information about each item, including images, product names, prices, quantities, and the option to remove items.

11.3.2 Checkout Page

The checkout page is where users provide their shipping and payment information. Bootstrap's form components can be helpful in designing this page.

```
<div class="container">

<div class="row">

<div class="col-md-6">

<!—Shipping Information—>

<h4>Shipping Information</h4>

<form>

<div class="form-group">

<label for="name">Name:</label>

<input type="text" class="form-control" id="name" placeholder="Full Name">

</div>

<!—Add more shipping fields (address, city, etc.)—>

</form>

</div>

<div class="col-md-6">

<!—Payment Information—>

<h4>Payment Information</h4>
```

```
<form>

<div class="form-group">

<label for="creditCard">Credit Card Number:</label>

<input type="text" class="form-control" id="creditCard" placeholder="Enter your card number">

</div>

<!—Add more payment fields (expiration date, CVV, etc.)—>

</form>

</div>

</div>

<!—Order Summary—>

<div class="order-summary">

<h4>Order Summary</h4>

<p>Subtotal: $99.98</p>

<p>Shipping: $5.00</p>

<h4>Total: $104.98</h4>

<button class="btn btn-success">Place Order</button>

</div>

</div>
```

Ensure that the checkout page is user-friendly, secure, and provides clear instructions for completing the purchase. Implementing validation for form fields is crucial to prevent errors during the checkout process.

11.3.3 Payment Gateways and Security

Integrate secure payment gateways to handle transactions. Ensure that your eCommerce website follows industry-standard security practices to protect user data and payment information.

11.3.4 Order Confirmation

After a successful purchase, provide users with an order confirmation page. Bootstrap's modal components can be used to display confirmation messages.

```
<!—Order Confirmation Modal—>

<div class="modal fade" id="orderConfirmationModal" tabindex="-1" role="dialog" aria-labelledby="orderConfirmationModalLabel" aria-hidden="true">

<!—Modal content—>

</div>
```

This modal can display order details and a thank-you message.

By effectively designing shopping cart and checkout pages, you can enhance the user experience and increase the likelihood of successful conversions on your Bootstrap-based eCommerce website. Next, we'll explore responsive product galleries in detail in the following section.

11.4 Responsive Product Galleries

Creating responsive product galleries is essential for providing users with an engaging visual experience on your Bootstrap-based eCommerce website. In this section, we'll explore techniques and best practices for designing product galleries that adapt to various screen sizes.

11.4.1 Using Bootstrap's Grid System

Bootstrap's grid system is a valuable tool for building responsive product galleries. You can organize product images into rows and columns to ensure they adjust gracefully to different device sizes.

```
<div class="row">

<div class="col-md-3 col-sm-6">

<img src="product1.jpg" alt="Product 1">

</div>

<div class="col-md-3 col-sm-6">

<img src="product2.jpg" alt="Product 2">

</div>

<!—Add more product items—>

</div>
```

By specifying different column classes for various screen sizes (e.g., col-md-3 and col-sm-6), you can control how many product images are displayed per row on different devices.

11.4.2 Implementing Image Thumbnails

Consider using image thumbnails to showcase multiple product images for each product. Bootstrap's thumbnail component can help create a visually appealing gallery.

```
<div class="row">

<div class="col-md-4">

<div class="thumbnail">

<img src="product1.jpg" alt="Product 1">

</div>

</div>

<div class="col-md-4">

<div class="thumbnail">

<img src="product2.jpg" alt="Product 2">

</div>

</div>

<!—Add more product items with thumbnails—>

</div>
```

Thumbnails allow users to click or tap on small images to view larger versions, enhancing the user experience.

11.4.3 Lightbox or Modal Pop-ups

Implementing lightbox or modal pop-ups for product images is a user-friendly approach. Bootstrap's modal component can be used to create these pop-ups.

<!—Product Image Modal—>

<**div class**="modal fade" **id**="productImageModal" **tabindex**="-1" **role**="dialog" **aria-labelledby**="productImageModalLabel" **aria-hidden**="true">

<!—Modal content with product image—>

</**div**>

When a user clicks on a product image thumbnail, you can use JavaScript to trigger the modal and display the larger image.

11.4.4 Mobile-Friendly Design

Ensure that your product galleries are mobile-friendly. Use responsive image classes like img-fluid to make sure images scale properly on smaller screens.

<**img src**="product.jpg" **class**="img-fluid" **alt**="Product Image">

Test the gallery on various devices to ensure a smooth and visually appealing experience for mobile users.

11.4.5 Lazy Loading for Performance

Consider implementing lazy loading for images within the gallery. Lazy loading loads images as the user scrolls, reducing initial page load times.

```
<img src="placeholder.jpg" data-src="product.jpg" class="img-fluid lazy" alt="Product Image">
```

JavaScript can be used to load the actual image source (data-src) when it comes into the viewport.

By following these best practices and utilizing Bootstrap's grid system and components, you can create responsive and visually appealing product galleries that enhance the user experience on your eCommerce website. Next, we'll explore payment forms and security considerations in more detail in the following section.

11.5 Payment Forms and Security

In this section, we'll delve into the crucial aspects of designing payment forms and ensuring security for your Bootstrap-based eCommerce website. A secure and user-friendly payment process is essential for gaining the trust of your customers and protecting their sensitive information.

11.5.1 Designing Payment Forms

Bootstrap provides various form components that can be used to create well-designed payment forms. Here's an example of a credit card payment form:

```
<form>

<div class="form-group">

<label for="cardNumber">Credit Card Number:</label>

<input type="text" class="form-control" id="cardNumber" placeholder="Enter your card number" required>

</div>
```

```
<div class="form-row">

<div class="col-md-6">

<label for="expiryDate">Expiry Date:</label>

<input type="text" class="form-control" id="expiryDate" placeholder="MM/YY" required>

</div>

<div class="col-md-6">

<label for="cvv">CVV:</label>

<input type="text" class="form-control" id="cvv" placeholder="CVV" required>

</div>

</div>

<div class="form-group">

<label for="cardHolder">Cardholder Name:</label>

<input type="text" class="form-control" id="cardHolder" placeholder="Enter cardholder name" required>

</div>

<button type="submit" class="btn btn-primary">Pay Now</button>

</form>
```

Ensure that payment forms are user-friendly, responsive, and intuitive. Proper field validation and error messages are essential to prevent user errors during the payment process.

11.5.2 Payment Gateway Integration

Integrate secure and reputable payment gateways to handle transactions on your eCommerce website. Popular payment gateways include PayPal, Stripe, and Square. These gateways provide APIs and documentation to facilitate integration.

<!—PayPal Button—>

<button class="btn btn-primary" **id**="paypal-button">Pay with PayPal</**button>**

You can use JavaScript to trigger the payment process when the user clicks the payment button.

11.5.3 SSL Encryption

Implement SSL (Secure Socket Layer) encryption to secure the data transmitted between the user's browser and your server. SSL certificates ensure that sensitive information, such as credit card numbers, is encrypted and protected during transmission.

11.5.4 PCI Compliance

Adhere to Payment Card Industry Data Security Standard (PCI DSS) requirements if you handle credit card information directly. PCI compliance ensures the secure storage and handling of cardholder data.

11.5.5 User Authentication

Implement user authentication to enhance security. Users should have unique accounts with strong passwords to access their payment information and order history.

11.5.6 Two-Factor Authentication (2FA)

Consider implementing two-factor authentication (2FA) for user accounts. 2FA adds an extra layer of security by requiring users to verify their identity through a second method, such as a one-time code sent to their mobile device.

11.5.7 Regular Security Audits

Regularly audit your website's security to identify and address vulnerabilities. Vulnerability scanning and penetration testing can help identify and mitigate potential threats.

11.5.8 Data Privacy Compliance

Ensure that your website complies with data privacy regulations, such as GDPR (General Data Protection Regulation) and CCPA (California Consumer Privacy Act), to protect user data and privacy rights.

By following these practices and integrating secure payment gateways, SSL encryption, and robust authentication mechanisms, you can build a secure and trustworthy payment process for your Bootstrap-based eCommerce website. Security should always be a top priority when handling customer payment information.

Chapter 12: Bootstrap for Content Management Systems

12.1 Integrating Bootstrap with WordPress

In this section, we'll explore how to integrate Bootstrap with WordPress, one of the most popular content management systems (CMS) in use today. WordPress provides a flexible and user-friendly platform for creating websites and blogs, and by incorporating Bootstrap, you can enhance the design and responsiveness of your WordPress site.

12.1.1 Understanding WordPress Themes

In the WordPress ecosystem, themes control the overall look and feel of a website. Themes are composed of template files, style sheets, and other assets. To integrate Bootstrap into WordPress, you can either create a custom theme or modify an existing one.

12.1.2 Creating a Custom WordPress Theme with Bootstrap

To create a custom WordPress theme with Bootstrap, follow these steps:

1. **Set Up Your Development Environment:** Install WordPress locally using software like XAMPP or WAMP, or use a hosting provider that supports WordPress development.
2. **Create a New Theme Directory:** Inside the WordPress wp-content/themes directory, create a new folder for your theme, e.g., my-bootstrap-theme.
3. **Create Theme Files:** Inside your theme folder, create

essential theme files such as style.css, index.php, and functions.php.

– In style.css, define your theme's information and dependencies, including Bootstrap stylesheets.

```
/*

Theme Name: My Bootstrap Theme

Description: A WordPress theme powered by Bootstrap.

Version: 1.0

Author: Your Name

Template: twentynineteen

*/

/* Enqueue Bootstrap styles */

function enqueue_bootstrap() {

wp_enqueue_style('bootstrap', 'https://stackpath.bootstrapcdn.com/bootstrap/4.5.2/css/bootstrap.min.css');

}

add_action('wp_enqueue_scripts', 'enqueue_bootstrap');
```

– In index.php, create the main template structure. You can use WordPress functions and template tags to retrieve and display content.

– In functions.php, enqueue Bootstrap and any additional scripts or styles required for your theme.

1. **Activate Your Theme:** Go to the WordPress Admin Dashboard, navigate to "Appearance" > "Themes," and activate your custom Bootstrap theme.

12.1.3 Using Bootstrap Components in WordPress

Once your Bootstrap-based theme is active, you can start utilizing Bootstrap components within your WordPress content. For example:

- To create responsive grids, you can use Bootstrap's grid classes directly in your post or page content.

```
<div class="row">

<div class="col-md-6">

<!—Content for the first column—>

</div>

<div class="col-md-6">

<!—Content for the second column—>

</div>

</div>
```

- You can incorporate Bootstrap navigation components, such as the Bootstrap navbar, into your site's header.

```
<nav class="navbar navbar-expand-lg navbar-light bg-light">
```

```
<a class="navbar-brand" href="#">My Website</a>

<!—Add navigation links and dropdowns here—>

</nav>
```

- Bootstrap's typography and styling classes can be applied to text and images in your WordPress posts and pages to maintain a consistent design.

By integrating Bootstrap with WordPress, you can leverage the power of a popular CMS while benefiting from the responsive and customizable features offered by Bootstrap. This combination allows you to create modern, mobile-friendly websites with ease.

12.2 Themes for Joomla and Drupal

In this section, we'll explore how to create themes for Joomla and Drupal, two other popular content management systems (CMS), and integrate Bootstrap into these themes. Both Joomla and Drupal provide powerful platforms for building websites and web applications, and incorporating Bootstrap can enhance their visual appeal and responsiveness.

12.2.1 Joomla Themes with Bootstrap

Creating a Joomla Bootstrap Theme

To create a Joomla theme with Bootstrap, you can follow these steps:

1. **Set Up Joomla:** Install Joomla on your local server or hosting environment if you haven't already.
2. **Create a New Theme Directory:** Inside the Joomla templates directory, create a new folder for your theme,

e.g., my-bootstrap-theme.

3. **Create Template Files:** Inside your theme folder, create essential template files, including index.php and templateDetails.xml. You may also need CSS and JavaScript files.

– In templateDetails.xml, define your theme's information and dependencies, including Bootstrap stylesheets.

```
<?xml version="1.0" encoding="utf-8"?>

<extension version="3.9" type="template">

<name>My Bootstrap Theme</name>

<creationDate>2023-01-01</creationDate>

<author>Your Name</author>

<description>A Joomla template powered by Bootstrap.</description>

<version>1.0</version>

<files>

<filename>index.php</filename>

</files>

<positions>

<!—Define module positions here—>
```

```
</positions>

<stylesheets>

<stylesheet>template.css</stylesheet>

<stylesheet>https://stackpath.bootstrapcdn.com/
bootstrap/4.5.2/css/bootstrap.min.css</stylesheet>

</stylesheets>

</extension>
```

– In index.php, create the main template structure and integrate Bootstrap classes as needed.

Using Bootstrap Components in Joomla

Once your Joomla Bootstrap theme is set up, you can utilize Bootstrap components in your Joomla articles and modules. For instance:

- To create responsive grids, you can apply Bootstrap's grid classes within your Joomla article content.

```
<div class="row">

<div class="col-md-6">

<!—Content for the first column—>

</div>

<div class="col-md-6">

<!—Content for the second column—>
```

```
</div>

</div>
```

- You can incorporate Bootstrap navigation components, like the Bootstrap navbar, into your Joomla template.

```
<nav class="navbar navbar-expand-lg navbar-light bg-light">

<a class="navbar-brand" href="#">My Joomla Website</a>

<!—Add navigation links and dropdowns here—>

</nav>
```

- Bootstrap's typography and styling classes can be applied to text and images within your Joomla articles to maintain a consistent design.

12.2.2 Drupal Themes with Bootstrap

Creating a Drupal Bootstrap Theme

To create a Drupal theme with Bootstrap, you can follow these steps:

1. **Set Up Drupal:** Install Drupal on your local server or hosting environment if you haven't already.
2. **Create a New Theme Directory:** Inside the Drupal themes directory, create a new folder for your theme, e.g., my_bootstrap_theme.
3. **Create Theme Files:** Inside your theme folder, create essential theme files, including my_bootstrap_theme.info.yml, my_bootstrap_theme.theme, and my_bootstrap_theme.libraries.yml. You may also need CSS

and JavaScript files.

– In my_bootstrap_theme.info.yml, define your theme's information and dependencies, including Bootstrap stylesheets.

name: 'My Bootstrap Theme'

type: theme

description: 'A Drupal theme powered by Bootstrap.'

core_version_requirement: ^8 || ^9

package: Custom

base theme: false

libraries:

- my_bootstrap_theme/global-styling

– In my_bootstrap_theme.libraries.yml, specify the libraries for your theme, including Bootstrap.

global-styling:

version: 1.x

css:

theme:

https://stackpath.bootstrapcdn.com/bootstrap/4.5.2/css/bootstrap.min.css: { type: external, minified: true }

– In my_bootstrap_theme.theme, create the main template structure and integrate Bootstrap classes as needed.

Using Bootstrap Components in Drupal

Once your Drupal Bootstrap theme is set up, you can utilize Bootstrap components in your Drupal content and templates. For example:

- To create responsive grids, you can apply Bootstrap's grid classes within your Drupal content.

```
<div class="row">
<div class="col-md-6">
<!—Content for the first column—>
</div>
<div class="col-md-6">
<!—Content for the second column—>
</div>
</div>
```

- You can incorporate Bootstrap navigation components, like the Bootstrap navbar, into your Drupal templates.

```
<nav class="navbar navbar-expand-lg navbar-light bg-light">
<a class="navbar-brand" href="#">My Drupal Website</a>
<!—Add navigation links and dropdowns here—>
```

</nav>

- Bootstrap's typography and styling classes can be applied to text and images within your Drupal content to maintain a consistent design.

By integrating Bootstrap with Joomla and Drupal, you can harness the power of these CMS platforms while benefiting from the responsive and customizable features offered by Bootstrap. This combination enables you to create modern, mobile-friendly websites and web applications with ease, catering to a wide range of user needs.

12.3 Custom Templates for CMS

In this section, we'll explore the creation of custom templates for content management systems (CMS) such as Joomla and Drupal. Custom templates allow you to have full control over the design and layout of your website or web application, including the integration of Bootstrap for responsive and stylish user interfaces.

12.3.1 Custom Joomla Templates

Creating a Custom Joomla Template

To create a custom Joomla template, follow these steps:

1. **Set Up Joomla:** Install Joomla on your local server or hosting environment if you haven't already.
2. **Create a New Template Directory:** Inside the Joomla templates directory, create a new folder for your template, e.g., my-custom-template.
3. **Define Template Files:** In your template folder, create

essential template files, including templateDetails.xml, index.php, and custom.css.

– In templateDetails.xml, define your template's information and dependencies.

```
<?xml version="1.0" encoding="utf-8"?>

<extension version="3.9" type="template">

<name>My Custom Template</name>

<creationDate>2023-01-01</creationDate>

<author>Your Name</author>

<description>A custom Joomla template.</description>

<version>1.0</version>

<files>

<filename>index.php</filename>

<filename>custom.css</filename>

</files>

</extension>
```

– In index.php, create the template's main structure and integrate Bootstrap classes and styles as needed.

Using Custom Joomla Templates with Bootstrap

Once your custom Joomla template is set up, you can utilize Bootstrap components and styles within your Joomla content and templates. For example:

- To create responsive grids, you can apply Bootstrap's grid classes within your Joomla articles and modules.

```
<div class="row">

<div class="col-md-6">

<!—Content for the first column—>

</div>

<div class="col-md-6">

<!—Content for the second column—>

</div>

</div>
```

- You can incorporate Bootstrap navigation components, such as the Bootstrap navbar, into your Joomla templates.

```
<nav class="navbar navbar-expand-lg navbar-light bg-light">

<a class="navbar-brand" href="#">My Joomla Website</a>

<!—Add navigation links and dropdowns here—>

</nav>
```

• Bootstrap's typography and styling classes can be applied to text and images within your Joomla articles to maintain a consistent design.

12.3.2 Custom Drupal Themes

Creating a Custom Drupal Theme

To create a custom Drupal theme, follow these steps:

1. **Set Up Drupal:** Install Drupal on your local server or hosting environment if you haven't already.
2. **Create a New Theme Directory:** Inside the Drupal themes directory, create a new folder for your theme, e.g., my_custom_theme.
3. **Define Theme Files:** In your theme folder, create essential theme files, including my_custom_theme.info.yml, my_custom_theme.theme, and my_custom_theme.libraries.yml. You may also need CSS and JavaScript files.

– In my_custom_theme.info.yml, define your theme's information and dependencies.

name: 'My Custom Theme'

type: theme

description: 'A custom Drupal theme.'

core_version_requirement: ^8 || ^9

package: Custom

base theme: false

libraries:

- my_custom_theme/global-styling

– In my_custom_theme.libraries.yml, specify the libraries for your theme, including Bootstrap.

global-styling:

version: 1.x

css:

theme:

https://stackpath.bootstrapcdn.com/bootstrap/4.5.2/css/bootstrap.min.css: { type: external, minified: true }

– In my_custom_theme.theme, create the theme's main structure and integrate Bootstrap classes and styles as needed.

Using Custom Drupal Themes with Bootstrap

Once your custom Drupal theme is set up, you can utilize Bootstrap components and styles within your Drupal content and templates in a manner similar to Joomla. For example:

- To create responsive grids, you can apply Bootstrap's grid classes within your Drupal content.

<div class="row"**>**

```
<div class="col-md-6">

<!—Content for the first column—>

</div>

<div class="col-md-6">

<!—Content for the second column—>

</div>

</div>
```

- You can incorporate Bootstrap navigation components, such as the Bootstrap navbar, into your Drupal templates.

```
<nav class="navbar navbar-expand-lg navbar-light bg-light">

<a class="navbar-brand" href="#">My Drupal Website</a>

<!—Add navigation links and dropdowns here—>

</nav>
```

- Bootstrap's typography and styling classes can be applied to text and images within your Drupal content to maintain a consistent design.

Creating custom templates for Joomla and Drupal gives you the freedom to design your website or web application exactly as you envision it. By integrating Bootstrap into these templates, you can ensure a responsive and visually appealing user experience across different devices and screen sizes.

12.4 Managing Content Responsively

In this section, we'll explore the importance of managing content responsibly in the context of Bootstrap and content management systems (CMS) like WordPress, Joomla, and Drupal. Responsively managing content involves creating web content that adapts well to various screen sizes and devices, ensuring a seamless user experience.

12.4.1 Responsive Typography

Responsive typography is a crucial aspect of content management. When working with Bootstrap and CMS platforms, consider the following practices for managing text:

- Use relative units like em and rem for font sizes to allow text to scale proportionally with the user's device.

```
body {
font-size: 1rem; /* Base font size */
}
h1 {
font-size: 2rem; /* Example header font size */
}
```

- Implement media queries to adjust font sizes and line spacing for different screen sizes. Bootstrap provides responsive typography classes like .text-sm, .text-md, and .text-lg that can be applied to elements.

• Prioritize legibility and readability by choosing appropriate fonts and line heights.

12.4.2 Responsive Images

Images are a significant part of web content. To ensure responsive images in your CMS-powered website:

• Use the img-fluid class in Bootstrap to make images scale with their parent containers and maintain their aspect ratios.

```
<img src="example.jpg" alt="Responsive Image" class="img-fluid">
```

• Provide multiple image sizes using the srcset attribute for better performance and user experience.

```
<img src="small.jpg" srcset="medium.jpg 800w, large.jpg 1200w" alt="Responsive Image">
```

• Utilize responsive image plugins and features offered by your CMS to automate image optimization and resizing.

12.4.3 Structured Content

Structure your content semantically using HTML5 elements like <header>, <article>, <section>, <aside>, and <footer>. This semantic structure helps screen readers and search engines understand your content and improves accessibility.

```
<article>

<header>

<h1>Article Title</h1>
```

```
</header>

<section>

<p>Article content goes here.</p>

</section>

<aside>

<p>Related information or links</p>

</aside>

<footer>

<p>Published on Date</p>

</footer>

</article>
```

12.4.4 Content Layout

Bootstrap's grid system makes it easy to create responsive content layouts. Consider the following practices:

- Use Bootstrap's grid classes (col-sm, col-md, col-lg, etc.) to arrange content in columns that adapt to different screen sizes.

```
<div class="row">

<div class="col-md-6">

<!—Content for the first column—>

</div>
```

```
<div class="col-md-6">

<!—Content for the second column—>

</div>

</div>
```

- Utilize Bootstrap's responsive utility classes to show or hide content based on screen size (d-sm-none, d-md-block, etc.).

- Test your content layout thoroughly on various devices to ensure it looks and functions as intended.

12.4.5 Accessibility

Accessibility is a critical aspect of content management. Ensure that your CMS-generated content is accessible by:

- Providing alternative text (alt attribute) for images to describe their content to users who rely on screen readers.

- Using semantic HTML elements and proper headings to structure content logically.

- Enabling accessibility features and plugins provided by your CMS to automate accessibility checks and improvements.

By following these practices, you can manage content responsibly within Bootstrap-based websites created with popular CMS platforms. Responsively managing content not only enhances user experience but also contributes to accessibility and SEO, ensuring your content reaches a wider audience across different devices and platforms.

12.5 Plugins and Extensions for CMS

In this section, we'll explore the world of plugins and extensions for content management systems (CMS) like WordPress, Joomla, and Drupal, with a focus on how they can enhance your Bootstrap-based websites. Plugins and extensions add functionality, features, and customization options to your CMS, allowing you to create versatile and powerful web experiences.

12.5.1 WordPress Plugins

Leveraging WordPress Plugins

WordPress offers a vast ecosystem of plugins that can extend the capabilities of your website. When working with Bootstrap-based WordPress themes, consider the following types of plugins:

- **Bootstrap Integration Plugins:** Some plugins are designed to seamlessly integrate Bootstrap into your WordPress theme. These plugins often include Bootstrap styles and scripts, making it easier to create responsive designs. Examples include "Bootstrap for WordPress" and "Bootstrap Shortcodes."

- **Page Builders:** Page builder plugins like Elementor, Beaver Builder, and Divi allow you to design custom page layouts and content with a drag-and-drop interface. Many of these builders offer Bootstrap compatibility for responsive designs.

- **Custom Post Types and Content Types:** Plugins like Custom Post Type UI and Advanced Custom Fields enable you to create custom content types and fields, making it easier to manage diverse content structures while maintaining a consistent design.

- **E-commerce Plugins:** If you're running an e-commerce website, plugins like WooCommerce can add robust shopping cart and product management features while ensuring Bootstrap compatibility.

- **SEO and Performance Plugins:** Enhance your website's SEO and performance with plugins like Yoast SEO and W3 Total Cache. These plugins can help optimize your Bootstrap-based site for search engines and speed.

12.5.2 Joomla Extensions

Extending Joomla with Bootstrap

Joomla also offers a range of extensions that can enhance your Bootstrap-powered Joomla website:

- **Template Frameworks:** Joomla template frameworks like Helix Ultimate and T3 Framework often include Bootstrap as a foundation, making it easier to create responsive and customizable templates.

- **Content Construction Kits (CCKs):** CCK extensions like K2 and Seblod allow you to create complex content structures, including custom fields and layouts, while ensuring compatibility with Bootstrap for responsive design.

- **Page Builders:** Joomla page builder extensions like SP Page Builder and Quix allow you to design and customize pages using Bootstrap-based elements and responsive layouts.

- **E-commerce Solutions:** For e-commerce websites, extensions like VirtueMart and HikaShop can provide robust online store functionality with Bootstrap compatibility.

- **SEO and Performance Extensions:** Improve SEO and website performance with Joomla extensions like SH404SEF and JCH Optimize, which help optimize your Bootstrap-based site for search engines and speed.

12.5.3 Drupal Modules

Enhancing Drupal with Modules

Drupal offers a rich collection of modules that can extend your Bootstrap-based Drupal website:

- **Base Themes:** Drupal base themes like Bootstrap and Barrio are specifically designed to work with Bootstrap, providing a solid foundation for creating responsive Drupal themes.

- **Content Construction Kit (CKEditor):** The CKEditor module allows you to integrate the CKEditor

WYSIWYG editor with Bootstrap styles, ensuring consistent content formatting.

- **Layout Builders:** Layout builder modules like Panels and Display Suite enable you to create custom page layouts and responsive designs with Bootstrap components.

- **E-commerce Modules:** If you're building an e-commerce site, modules like Drupal Commerce can provide extensive e-commerce functionality while allowing you to maintain Bootstrap compatibility.

- **SEO and Performance Modules:** Improve SEO and website performance with Drupal modules like Metatag and Advanced CSS/JS Aggregation, which help optimize your Bootstrap-based site for search engines and speed.

12.5.4 Installation and Management

When using plugins and extensions with your CMS, it's essential to install and manage them correctly:

- **Installation:** Most CMSs offer straightforward installation processes for plugins and extensions. Typically, you can upload the plugin's ZIP file through the CMS admin interface and activate it.

- **Compatibility:** Ensure that the plugins or extensions you choose are compatible with your CMS version and Bootstrap framework. Check for updates regularly to stay up to date.

- **Security:** Download plugins and extensions from reputable sources, such as the official CMS repositories or trusted developers. Avoid using pirated or unverified extensions, as they can pose security risks.

By leveraging plugins and extensions, you can enhance the functionality, design, and performance of your Bootstrap-based websites on popular CMS platforms. These extensions can save you time and effort while providing a wealth of customization options to meet your specific web development needs.

Chapter 13: Animation and Transitions

13.1 CSS Animations with Bootstrap

Bootstrap provides a range of utility classes and components for adding CSS animations to your web projects. CSS animations can enhance user experience by adding subtle or eye-catching motion to various elements on your page. In this section, we'll explore how to leverage Bootstrap for CSS animations.

13.1.1 Using Bootstrap Animation Classes

Bootstrap offers a set of predefined CSS animation classes that you can apply to elements in your HTML. These classes are part of the animate__ namespace and are designed to work seamlessly with the Bootstrap framework. Here are some commonly used animation classes:

- animate__animated: This class is the foundation for applying animations. You should use it in conjunction with other animation classes.

- animate__fadeIn: This class fades an element in with a smooth opacity transition.

- animate__fadeOut: This class fades an element out with a smooth opacity transition.

- animate__slideInLeft: This class slides an element into view from the left.

- animate__slideInRight: This class slides an element into view from the right.

- animate__rotateIn: This class adds a rotation effect to an element, making it appear to rotate while fading in.

Here's an example of how to use these animation classes in HTML:

<div class="animate__animated animate__fadeIn">

<!—Content to be animated—>

</div>

You can combine multiple animation classes to create complex animations. For instance, to create an element that slides in from the left while fading in, you can use both animate__slideInLeft and animate__fadeIn classes together.

13.1.2 Customizing Animation Duration and Delay

Bootstrap allows you to customize the duration and delay of CSS animations using additional classes. These classes are part of the animate__ namespace as well:

- animate__fast: Speeds up the animation duration.
- animate__slow: Slows down the animation duration.
- animate__delay-{duration}: Delays the start of the animation by the specified duration (e.g., animate__delay-1s for a 1-second delay).

You can combine these classes with your chosen animation classes to control the speed and timing of animations. For example:

<div class="animate__animated animate__fadeIn animate__slow animate__delay-2s">

```
<!—Content to be animated—>

</div>
```

This combination creates an element that fades in slowly with a 2-second delay.

13.1.3 Triggering Animations

By default, Bootstrap animations trigger when the page loads. However, you can also trigger animations based on user interactions, such as hover or click events, by using JavaScript. To do this, you'll need to add and remove animation classes dynamically using JavaScript event listeners.

For example, you can use JavaScript to apply an animation class when a button is clicked:

```
<button id="animateButton">Animate</button>

<div id="animatedElement">

<!—Content to be animated—>

</div>

document.getElementById("animateButton").addEventListener("click",
function () {

const animatedElement =
document.getElementById("animatedElement");

animatedElement.classList.add("animate__animated",
"animate__bounce");

// Remove the animation class after the animation completes
```

```
animatedElement.addEventListener("animationend", function () {

animatedElement.classList.remove("animate__animated", "animate__bounce");

});

});
```

In this example, when the "Animate" button is clicked, the animate__bounce animation class is added to the target element (animatedElement). The animationend event listener removes the animation class after the animation finishes, allowing you to trigger the animation again if desired.

Bootstrap's animation classes and customization options make it easy to add engaging CSS animations to your website without writing extensive CSS or JavaScript code. These animations can improve user engagement and provide a more visually appealing user experience.

13.2 Transition Effects for Interactive Elements

Bootstrap also provides a range of classes and components for adding transition effects to interactive elements on your web pages. Transition effects can make user interactions more engaging and provide visual feedback when users interact with buttons, links, and other UI elements. In this section, we'll explore how to use Bootstrap for adding transition effects.

13.2.1 Using Bootstrap Transition Classes

Bootstrap offers a set of transition classes that you can apply to elements to control how they animate during certain actions or interactions. These classes are typically used in combination with pseudo-classes like :hover, :focus, and :active. Here are some commonly used transition classes:

- fade: This class provides a smooth fade-in and fade-out effect. It's often used with buttons and links to create subtle transitions when they are hovered over or clicked.

```
<a href="#" class="btn btn-primary fade">Hover Me</a>
```

- btn-outline-{color}: Bootstrap's button classes can be used with transition classes to create outline buttons with transition effects. For example, btn-outline-primary creates a primary color outline button.

```
<a href="#" class="btn btn-outline-primary fade">Hover Me</a>
```

- btn-sm and btn-lg: You can combine these button size classes with transition classes to create buttons with different sizes that transition smoothly.

```
<a href="#" class="btn btn-primary btn-lg fade">Large Button</a>
```

13.2.2 Creating Custom Transitions

Bootstrap also allows you to create custom transition effects using CSS. This is useful when you want to achieve unique animations for specific elements. Here's an example of creating a custom transition effect for a card element:

```
<div class="card custom-transition">

<div class="card-body">

<h5 class="card-title">Custom Transition</h5>

<p class="card-text">This card has a custom transition effect.</p>
```

```
</div>

</div>

.custom-transition {

transition: transform 0.3s ease-in-out;

}

.custom-transition:hover {

transform: scale(1.05);

}
```

In this example, we've defined a custom CSS class custom-transition that specifies a transition effect on the transform property. When the card is hovered over, it scales up slightly, creating a custom transition effect.

13.2.3 Using Bootstrap's Collapse Component

Bootstrap includes a collapse component that provides smooth transitions for expanding and collapsing content. This component is often used for creating accordions, collapsible panels, and dropdown menus.

To use the collapse component, you'll need to include the appropriate Bootstrap JavaScript and CSS files and use the data-toggle and data-target attributes on your HTML elements. Here's an example of creating a simple collapsible panel:

```
<button class="btn btn-primary" type="button" data-toggle="collapse" data-target="#collapseExample">

Toggle Panel
```

```
</button>

<div class="collapse" id="collapseExample">

<div class="card card-body">

This is a collapsible panel. Click the button above to toggle it.

</div>

</div>
```

In this example, clicking the “Toggle Panel” button will smoothly expand or collapse the content inside the collapseExample element.

Bootstrap’s transition and collapse classes and components make it easy to add interactive and visually appealing effects to your web pages. These effects can improve user engagement and make your website more interactive and user-friendly.

13.3 Animating Modals and Alerts

Bootstrap allows you to create animated modals and alerts, enhancing the user experience by providing engaging and informative visual effects. In this section, we’ll explore how to animate modals and alerts using Bootstrap.

13.3.1 Animated Modals

Modals are commonly used for displaying additional content, forms, or messages without navigating away from the current page. Bootstrap provides the modal component for creating modals, and you can add animation to them for a more polished appearance.

To animate a modal, you can use Bootstrap’s built-in CSS classes and JavaScript events. Here’s an example of creating an animated modal:

```
<!—Button to trigger the modal—>

<button type="button" class="btn btn-primary" data-toggle="modal" data-target="#myModal">

Open Modal

</button>

<!—The Modal—>

<div class="modal fade" id="myModal">

<div class="modal-dialog modal-dialog-centered">

<div class="modal-content">

<!—Modal Header—>

<div class="modal-header">

<h4 class="modal-title">Animated Modal</h4>

<button type="button" class="close" data-dismiss="modal">&times;</button>

</div>

<!—Modal body—>

<div class="modal-body">

This is an animated modal. You can add content here.

</div>

<!—Modal footer—>

<div class="modal-footer">
```

```
<button type="button" class="btn btn-secondary" data-dismiss="modal">Close</button>

</div>

</div>

</div>

</div>
```

In this example, the modal has the class fade, which adds a fading animation when it appears and disappears. The data-toggle and data-target attributes on the button trigger the modal. When the "Open Modal" button is clicked, the modal fades in, and when the close button is clicked or the backdrop is clicked, it fades out.

You can further customize the animation by modifying the CSS and JavaScript according to your preferences.

13.3.2 Animated Alerts

Alerts are often used to display important messages or notifications to users. You can animate Bootstrap alerts to draw attention to them using CSS animations.

Here's an example of creating an animated alert:

```
<div class="alert alert-info fade show">

<button type="button" class="close" data-dismiss="alert">&times;</button>

This is an animated alert. Click the close button to dismiss it.

</div>
```

In this example, the alert has the class fade to add a fading animation when it appears. The show class is used to initially display the alert. You can dismiss the alert by clicking the close button (×), which is achieved using the data-dismiss attribute.

13.3.3 Customizing Animations

You can customize the animations of modals and alerts by overriding Bootstrap's default styles and using CSS animations and transitions. By modifying the CSS, you can create different animation effects, such as sliding, bouncing, or fading.

For modals, you can target elements like .modal.fade, .modal.show, and .modal-dialog to customize their animations. For alerts, you can target elements like .alert.fade, .alert.show, and .close for animation customization.

Remember to test and fine-tune your animations to ensure they match your website's design and provide a smooth and visually appealing user experience.

Animating modals and alerts in Bootstrap can help improve user engagement and provide a more interactive interface. By adding subtle animations to these elements, you can make your website or web application feel more dynamic and polished.

13.4 Scroll Animations and Reveal Effects

Scroll animations and reveal effects are popular techniques used in web design to add interactivity and engagement to web pages. These effects trigger animations when elements come into view as the user scrolls down the page. In this section, we'll explore how to implement scroll animations and reveal effects using Bootstrap and other web technologies.

13.4.1 Implementing Scroll Animations

Scroll animations are often used to create eye-catching effects as users scroll through a web page. These animations can include fading in elements, sliding elements into view, or scaling elements up as they become visible in the viewport.

To implement scroll animations, you can use a combination of HTML, CSS, and JavaScript. Bootstrap provides a solid foundation for structuring your content and can be enhanced with additional JavaScript libraries like ScrollReveal or AOS (Animate On Scroll).

Here's a basic example of how to create a scroll animation using Bootstrap and the AOS library:

```
<!DOCTYPE html>

<html lang="en">

<head>

<meta charset="UTF-8">

<meta name="viewport" content="width=device-width, initial-scale=1.0">

<link rel="stylesheet" href="https://cdn.jsdelivr.net/npm/bootstrap/dist/css/bootstrap.min.css">

<link rel="stylesheet" href="https://cdn.jsdelivr.net/npm/aos@2.3.1/dist/aos.css">

<title>Scroll Animation Example</title>

</head>

<body>
```

```
<div class="container mt-5">
<div class="row">
<div class="col-md-6">
<h1 data-aos="fade-up">Scroll Animation</h1>
<p data-aos="fade-up" data-aos-delay="200">Add scroll animations to your web page with Bootstrap and AOS.</p>
</div>
<div class="col-md-6">
<img src="image.jpg" alt="Animated Image" data-aos="fade-left" data-aos-delay="400">
</div>
</div>
</div>
<script src="https://cdn.jsdelivr.net/npm/bootstrap/dist/js/bootstrap.min.js"></script>
<script src="https://cdn.jsdelivr.net/npm/aos@2.3.1/dist/aos.js"></script>
<script>
AOS.init();
</script>
</body>
</html>
```

In this example, we've included Bootstrap for layout and styling and the AOS library for scroll animations. Elements with the data-aos attribute are animated when they come into view during scrolling. You can control the animation type and delay using these attributes.

13.4.2 Reveal Effects with ScrollSpy

Bootstrap's ScrollSpy component can be used to trigger reveal effects as users scroll down the page and specific sections or elements become visible in the viewport. ScrollSpy highlights the corresponding navigation links and triggers custom JavaScript functions when elements are scrolled into view.

To implement reveal effects with Bootstrap ScrollSpy, you'll need to set up the navigation structure and JavaScript code. Here's a simplified example:

```
<!DOCTYPE html>

<html lang="en">

<head>

<meta charset="UTF-8">

<meta name="viewport" content="width=device-width, initial-scale=1.0">

<link rel="stylesheet" href="https://cdn.jsdelivr.net/npm/bootstrap/dist/css/bootstrap.min.css">

<title>Reveal Effects Example</title>

</head>

<body data-spy="scroll" data-target="#navbar">
```

```
<nav id="navbar" class="navbar navbar-expand-lg navbar-light bg-light">

<ul class="navbar-nav">

<li class="nav-item">

<a class="nav-link" href="#section1">Section 1</a>

</li>

<li class="nav-item">

<a class="nav-link" href="#section2">Section 2</a>

</li>

<li class="nav-item">

<a class="nav-link" href="#section3">Section 3</a>

</li>

</ul>

</nav>

<div id="section1" class="container mt-5">

<h1>Section 1</h1>

<p>This is the first section.</p>

</div>

<div id="section2" class="container mt-5">

<h1>Section 2</h1>

<p>This is the second section.</p>
```

```
</div>

<div id="section3" class="container mt-5">

<h1>Section 3</h1>

<p>This is the third section.</p>

</div>

<script src="https://cdn.jsdelivr.net/npm/bootstrap/dist/js/bootstrap.min.js"></script>

</body>

</html>
```

In this example, we've set up a navigation bar with links that point to different sections on the page. The data-spy and data-target attributes are used to enable ScrollSpy functionality. As users scroll, the corresponding navigation link is highlighted, creating a reveal effect for the current section.

You can further customize the appearance and behavior of the reveal effects using CSS and JavaScript to achieve your desired visual effects and interactivity.

13.5 Performance Considerations

When implementing animations and transitions in your Bootstrap-based web projects, it's essential to consider performance to ensure that your website runs smoothly and provides a great user experience. In this section, we'll explore some performance considerations and best practices for using animations and transitions effectively.

13.5.1 Limit the Number of Animations

While animations and transitions can add visual appeal to your website, using too many of them can negatively impact performance. Each animation or transition consumes CPU and memory resources, and excessive use can lead to slow page rendering and sluggish user interactions.

To maintain good performance, limit the number of animations and transitions on a page. Focus on using them strategically to highlight key elements or provide user feedback rather than animating every element.

13.5.2 Use Hardware Acceleration

Modern web browsers can take advantage of hardware acceleration to optimize animations and transitions. When an animation is hardware-accelerated, it offloads the rendering process to the computer's GPU (Graphics Processing Unit), resulting in smoother and more efficient animations.

To enable hardware acceleration, ensure that your animations use CSS properties that are GPU-accelerated. Common properties that can be accelerated include transform, opacity, scale, and translate. By applying animations to these properties, you can take advantage of hardware acceleration.

13.5.3 Optimize Animation Performance

Optimizing animation performance involves several strategies:

- **Use CSS Transforms:** Whenever possible, use CSS transforms (e.g., translate, rotate, scale) for animations. Transforms are typically hardware-accelerated and provide smoother animations.

- **Reduce Redraws:** Minimize changes to properties that trigger expensive redraws, such as layout or paint operations. Changes to the width, height, or position properties can be performance-intensive.

- **Use requestAnimationFrame:** JavaScript animations should use the requestAnimationFrame method for smoother performance. It helps synchronize animations with the browser's rendering cycle.

```
function animate() {

// Your animation logic here

requestAnimationFrame(animate);

}

animate(); // Start the animation loop
```

- **Debounce and Throttle Animations:** When handling scroll events that trigger animations, consider debouncing or throttling the event handlers to avoid excessive animations while scrolling.

13.5.4 Optimize Images and Media

Animations that involve images or multimedia content can significantly impact page load times. To ensure smooth performance:

- **Optimize Images:** Compress and optimize images to reduce their file size without compromising quality. Use responsive image techniques to load appropriately sized images for different devices and screen sizes.

- **Lazy Loading:** Implement lazy loading for images and multimedia content that are not initially visible on the screen. Lazy loading loads assets as the user scrolls down the page, reducing the initial page load time.

- **Video and Audio Compression:** Compress video and audio files to reduce their size. Consider using modern video formats like WebM and audio formats like Opus for better compression.

13.5.5 Test on Various Devices and Browsers

Always test your animations and transitions on a variety of devices and web browsers. Different browsers and devices may handle animations differently, and what works well in one environment may not perform as expected in another.

Perform cross-browser testing to ensure that your animations and transitions are compatible with popular browsers like Chrome, Firefox, Safari, and Edge. Use responsive design principles to ensure that animations adapt to different screen sizes and orientations.

By following these performance considerations and best practices, you can create visually appealing animations and transitions in your Bootstrap-based web projects while maintaining excellent performance and a seamless user experience.

Chapter 14: Bootstrap in Single Page Applications

14.1 SPA Frameworks and Bootstrap

Single Page Applications (SPAs) have gained popularity for their seamless and dynamic user experiences. SPAs are web applications that load a single HTML page and dynamically update content as users interact with the application. They often rely on client-side JavaScript frameworks and libraries to achieve this behavior. In this section, we'll explore how Bootstrap can be integrated into SPA frameworks and the benefits of using Bootstrap in SPAs.

14.1.1 SPA Frameworks Overview

SPA frameworks like React, Angular, and Vue.js are commonly used for building modern web applications. These frameworks allow developers to create interactive and responsive user interfaces by handling routing, state management, and UI updates on the client side.

Bootstrap, with its extensive library of CSS components and JavaScript plugins, can complement SPA frameworks by providing a consistent and visually appealing design system. Integrating Bootstrap into SPAs ensures that your application maintains a polished and user-friendly appearance while benefiting from the framework's flexibility.

14.1.2 Benefits of Using Bootstrap in SPAs

Consistency and Design Patterns

Bootstrap offers a set of design patterns and pre-built UI components that help maintain a consistent look and feel across your SPA. By adhering to Bootstrap's design principles, you can ensure that your application follows best practices in terms of layout, typography, and responsive design.

Rapid Prototyping

Bootstrap's UI components allow for rapid prototyping in SPAs. You can quickly create user interfaces, forms, navigation menus, and modals without the need to build everything from scratch. This speeds up development and allows you to focus on the application's core functionality.

Responsive Design

Bootstrap's responsive grid system and utility classes make it easier to create SPAs that adapt to various screen sizes and devices. This is crucial for delivering a seamless user experience across desktops, tablets, and mobile devices.

Extensibility

Bootstrap is highly extensible, allowing you to customize and extend its components to match the unique requirements of your SPA. Whether you need to create custom themes, modify existing components, or add new functionality, Bootstrap provides a solid foundation for customization.

Community and Documentation

Bootstrap has a large and active community of developers, which means you can find plenty of resources, tutorials, and third-party plugins to enhance your SPA. Bootstrap's official documentation is comprehensive and provides guidance on using Bootstrap with various JavaScript frameworks.

14.1.3 Integrating Bootstrap with SPA Frameworks

Integrating Bootstrap with SPA frameworks typically involves the following steps:

1. **Installation:** Include Bootstrap's CSS and JavaScript files in your SPA project. You can do this by linking to Bootstrap's CDN (Content Delivery Network) or by using package managers like npm or yarn.
2. **Component Integration:** Use Bootstrap's CSS classes and HTML structure to build UI components within your SPA framework. For example, you can create navigation menus, forms, buttons, and modals using Bootstrap components.
3. **Customization:** Customize Bootstrap's styles and components to match your SPA's design requirements. You can override Bootstrap's default styles using custom CSS or by leveraging the framework's theming capabilities.
4. **JavaScript Interactions:** Utilize Bootstrap's JavaScript plugins for interactive components like modals, tooltips, and dropdowns. Ensure that these components are integrated seamlessly with your SPA's logic and routing.
5. **Responsiveness:** Leverage Bootstrap's responsive grid system to design layouts that adapt to different screen sizes. Use media queries and Bootstrap's utility classes to fine-

tune responsive behavior.

6. **Testing and Optimization:** Thoroughly test your SPA with Bootstrap components across various browsers and devices. Optimize the performance by minimizing unnecessary CSS and JavaScript to reduce load times.

By following these integration steps, you can harness the power of Bootstrap to enhance the user interface of your SPA while taking full advantage of your chosen framework's capabilities for building dynamic and responsive applications.

14.2 Routing and Navigation in SPAs

One of the fundamental aspects of Single Page Applications (SPAs) is routing and navigation. SPAs rely on client-side routing to load and display different views or components without refreshing the entire page. In this section, we'll explore how Bootstrap can be used in conjunction with SPA routing and navigation systems and provide insights into best practices.

14.2.1 SPA Routing Basics

SPA routing is managed on the client side using JavaScript frameworks and libraries like React Router, Vue Router, or Angular Router. These routing solutions allow you to define routes, associate them with specific components, and handle navigation between them.

Bootstrap comes into play by providing navigation components like navbars, navigation menus, and pagination that can seamlessly integrate with your SPA's routing system.

14.2.2 Bootstrap Navigation Components

Bootstrap offers a range of navigation components that can enhance the user experience in SPAs:

Navbars

Bootstrap's navbar component provides a flexible and customizable way to create navigation bars for your SPA. You can include navigation links, dropdown menus, branding elements, and responsive behavior.

Here's an example of using Bootstrap's navbar with React Router:

```
import { Link } from 'react-router-dom';

function Navbar() {

return (

<nav className="navbar navbar-expand-lg navbar-light bg-light">

<Link className="navbar-brand" to="/">SPA App</Link>

<button className="navbar-toggler" type="button" data-toggle="collapse" data-target="#navbarNav" aria-controls="navbarNav" aria-expanded="false" aria-label="Toggle navigation">

<span className="navbar-toggler-icon"></span>

</button>

<div className="collapse navbar-collapse" id="navbarNav">

<ul className="navbar-nav">
```

```
<li className="nav-item">
<Link className="nav-link" to="/">Home</Link>
</li>
<li className="nav-item">
<Link className="nav-link" to="/about">About</Link>
</li>
<li className="nav-item">
<Link className="nav-link" to="/contact">Contact</Link>
</li>
</ul>
</div>
</nav>
);
}
export default Navbar;
```

In this example, the Link component from React Router is used to create navigation links that change the route without causing a full page reload.

Breadcrumbs

Bootstrap's breadcrumb component is useful for displaying the user's current location within the SPA's hierarchical structure. It can be integrated with your SPA routing to show the user's path through different views.

```
import { Link } from 'react-router-dom';

function Breadcrumbs() {

return (

<nav aria-label="breadcrumb">

<ol className="breadcrumb">

<li className="breadcrumb-item"><Link to="/">Home</Link></li>

<li className="breadcrumb-item"><Link to="/products">Products</Link></li>

<li className="breadcrumb-item active" aria-current="page">Product Details</li>

</ol>

</nav>

);

}

export default Breadcrumbs;
```

Pagination

If your SPA displays paginated content, Bootstrap's pagination component can be integrated with your routing system to handle page changes.

```
import { Link } from 'react-router-dom';

function Pagination({ currentPage, totalPages }) {

const pages = Array.from({ length: totalPages }, (_, i) => i + 1);

return (

<nav aria-label="Page navigation">

<ul className="pagination">

{pages.map((page) => (

<li className={`page-item ${page === currentPage ? 'active' : ''}`} key={page}>

<Link to={`/products?page=${page}`} className="page-link">{page}</Link>

</li>

))}

</ul>

</nav>

);

}

export default Pagination;
```

14.2.3 Best Practices for SPA Routing and Bootstrap

To effectively integrate Bootstrap navigation components into your SPA, consider the following best practices:

- **Consistent Navigation:** Ensure that navigation elements such as navbars and breadcrumbs are consistently styled across your SPA. Bootstrap's predefined styles can help maintain a cohesive design.

- **Active Links:** Use Bootstrap's active class or equivalent classes from your SPA framework to indicate the active route in navigation menus. This helps users understand their current location within the SPA.

- **Responsive Design:** Make sure navigation components are responsive and adapt to different screen sizes. Bootstrap provides responsive classes that can be applied to navigation elements.

- **Optimize Loading:** Use route-based code splitting or lazy loading techniques provided by your SPA framework to optimize the loading of components. This prevents unnecessary resource loading when navigating between routes.

- **Route Guarding:** If your SPA requires authentication or authorization, use route guards provided by your SPA framework to protect routes. Bootstrap components can be integrated seamlessly with protected routes.

By following these best practices, you can effectively integrate Bootstrap navigation components into your SPA's routing system, providing users with an intuitive and visually appealing navigation experience while maintaining the benefits of client-side routing.

14.3 State Management with Bootstrap UI

State management is a critical aspect of building Single Page Applications (SPAs). It involves handling the application's data and ensuring that changes to the data are reflected in the user interface. While Bootstrap is primarily a CSS and UI library, it can still play a role in state management when used in conjunction with JavaScript frameworks and libraries. In this section, we'll explore how Bootstrap UI components can be integrated with state management in SPAs.

14.3.1 Understanding State Management in SPAs

In SPAs, state management typically involves managing the application's data, user interface, and user interactions. JavaScript frameworks like React, Angular, and Vue.js provide their own state management solutions, such as React's state, Redux, or Vuex. These tools allow you to define, update, and synchronize the application's state across different components.

Bootstrap, on the other hand, offers a wide range of UI components like forms, buttons, modals, and tooltips that can be used to build the user interface of your SPA. These components can be dynamic and interactive, and their behavior often depends on the underlying application state.

14.3.2 Interaction Between Bootstrap UI and Application State

Integrating Bootstrap UI components with your application's state involves making the UI components responsive to changes in the state. Here are some common scenarios:

Form Controls

Bootstrap's form controls like input fields, checkboxes, and radio buttons can be bound to application state variables. When the user interacts with these controls, the state is updated accordingly. For example, in a React-based SPA, you can use controlled components to achieve this:

```
import React, { useState } from 'react';

function MyForm() {

const [name, setName] = useState('');

const handleNameChange = (event) => {

setName(event.target.value);

};

return (

<form>

<div className="form-group">

<label htmlFor="name">Name</label>

<input

type="text"

className="form-control"

id="name"

value={name}
```

```
onChange={handleNameChange}

/>

</div>

</form>

);

}

export default MyForm;
```

In this example, the name input field is controlled by the name state variable, and changes in the input field are reflected in the state.

Modals and Popovers

Bootstrap modals and popovers can be triggered and controlled based on the application state. For instance, you might show a modal when a specific condition in your SPA's state is met. You can use conditional rendering or state management libraries to achieve this behavior.

```
import React, { useState } from 'react';

function MyModal() {

const [showModal, setShowModal] = useState(false);

const openModal = () => {

setShowModal(true);

};

const closeModal = () => {
```

```
setShowModal(false);
};
return (
<div>
<button onClick={openModal}>Open Modal</button>
{showModal && (
<div className="modal">
<div className="modal-content">
<span className="close" onClick={closeModal}>&times;</span>
<p>Modal content goes here.</p>
</div>
</div>
)}
</div>
);
}
export default MyModal;
```

In this React example, the modal is shown or hidden based on the value of the showModal state variable.

Tooltips and Popovers

Bootstrap tooltips and popovers can provide additional information or actions when the user interacts with specific elements. You can conditionally show or hide these components based on the application state. JavaScript frameworks often provide mechanisms for handling such interactions.

```
import React, { useState } from 'react';

function MyComponent() {

const [showTooltip, setShowTooltip] = useState(false);

const toggleTooltip = () => {

setShowTooltip(!showTooltip);

};

return (

<div>

<button

onClick={toggleTooltip}

onMouseEnter={() => setShowTooltip(true)}

onMouseLeave={() => setShowTooltip(false)}

>

Hover me

</button>
```

```
{showTooltip && (
<div className="tooltip">
This is a tooltip.
</div>
)}
</div>
);
}
export default MyComponent;
```

In this React example, the tooltip is shown or hidden based on the showTooltip state variable, which is updated when the user hovers over or clicks the button.

14.3.3 Best Practices for Bootstrap UI and State Management

To effectively integrate Bootstrap UI components with state management in SPAs, consider the following best practices:

- **Component Composition:** Break down your UI into small, reusable components. This makes it easier to manage the state associated with each component and promotes a more modular codebase.
- **Use Controlled Components:** For form controls, use controlled components to bind UI elements to application state. This ensures that changes in the UI are reflected in the state and vice versa.

- **Conditional Rendering:** Use conditional rendering to show or hide Bootstrap UI components based on the application state. JavaScript frameworks provide mechanisms for conditional rendering.

- **State Management Libraries:** If your SPA is complex and requires global state management, consider using state management libraries like Redux (for React), Vuex (for Vue.js), or NgRx (for Angular). These libraries help manage application-wide state efficiently.

- **Optimize Rerendering:** Be mindful of unnecessary rerendering. Some state changes may not require a full rerender of the component tree. Use shouldComponentUpdate (in React) or similar mechanisms in other frameworks to optimize rendering.

By following these best practices, you can ensure that Bootstrap UI components and your application state work together seamlessly, providing an interactive and responsive user interface in your SPA.

14.4 Optimizing Load Times and Performance

Performance optimization is a crucial aspect of building Single Page Applications (SPAs) that deliver a seamless user experience. Optimizing load times and overall performance ensures that your SPA loads quickly and responds smoothly to user interactions. In this section, we'll explore various techniques for optimizing the performance of SPAs that use Bootstrap UI components.

14.4.1 Minimizing Initial Page Load

The initial load time of your SPA is critical for user engagement. Users expect web pages to load quickly, and long loading times can lead to higher bounce rates. Here are some strategies to minimize the initial page load:

Code Splitting

Use code splitting techniques provided by your SPA framework to split your application's code into smaller, more manageable chunks. This allows you to load only the necessary code for the initial route and lazy-load additional code as the user navigates through the application. Code splitting reduces the initial load time and speeds up the first interaction.

Lazy Loading

Lazy loading is a technique that defers the loading of non-essential resources, such as images, scripts, and data, until they are needed. For example, you can implement lazy loading for images below the fold, ensuring that they are loaded as the user scrolls down the page. This reduces the initial page load size and improves perceived performance.

Minification and Compression

Minify your JavaScript and CSS files to remove unnecessary whitespace, comments, and reduce file size. Additionally, enable server-side compression (e.g., GZIP) to compress responses before they are sent to the client. Smaller file sizes result in faster downloads and rendering.

14.4.2 Caching Strategies

Caching can significantly improve load times for returning users by reducing the need to re-download resources. Implementing caching strategies is essential for SPA performance:

Browser Caching

Leverage browser caching by setting appropriate cache headers for your assets. This instructs the user's browser to store and reuse assets locally, reducing the need for repeated downloads. You can control caching behavior for different asset types, such as images, stylesheets, and scripts.

Service Workers

Service workers are scripts that run in the background and intercept network requests. They enable more advanced caching strategies, such as caching assets for offline use or serving cached assets when the network is slow. Service workers are particularly valuable for Progressive Web Apps (PWAs) built with SPAs.

14.4.3 Optimizing Images and Media

Images and media assets can significantly impact load times. To optimize them:

Image Compression

Compress and resize images to reduce their file size while maintaining acceptable quality. Use image optimization tools or online services to automatically compress images before deploying them to your SPA.

Responsive Images

Implement responsive image techniques to serve different image sizes based on the user's device and screen resolution. Use the <picture> element or srcset attribute to specify multiple image sources, ensuring that the browser loads the most appropriate image.

Lazy Loading Images

As mentioned earlier, lazy loading can be applied to images to delay their loading until they become visible in the user's viewport. This technique improves initial page load times and reduces unnecessary image downloads.

14.4.4 JavaScript Optimization

JavaScript plays a significant role in the interactivity of SPAs. Optimizing JavaScript can lead to improved performance:

Bundle Splitting

If your SPA uses a build tool like Webpack, consider using bundle splitting to create separate bundles for different parts of your application. This allows you to load only the JavaScript code required for the current route, reducing the initial load time.

Tree Shaking

Tree shaking is a technique used by modern JavaScript bundlers to eliminate unused code from your bundles. Ensure that your build process includes tree shaking to remove any dead code, resulting in smaller JavaScript bundles.

Code Splitting for Third-party Libraries

If your SPA relies on third-party libraries, use code splitting to load them on-demand rather than including them in the initial bundle. Loading third-party libraries only when needed can significantly reduce the initial load time.

14.4.5 Content Delivery Networks (CDNs)

Consider using Content Delivery Networks (CDNs) to distribute your assets geographically closer to your users. CDNs cache and serve your assets from servers located in multiple regions, reducing latency and load times for users accessing your SPA from different parts of the world.

14.4.6 Profiling and Testing

Regularly profile and test your SPA's performance using browser developer tools and performance monitoring tools. Identify bottlenecks, slow-loading resources, and areas for improvement. Conduct testing on various devices and network conditions to ensure consistent performance.

By implementing these performance optimization techniques, you can enhance the speed and responsiveness of your SPA that utilizes Bootstrap UI components. A fast-loading and smooth-running SPA contributes to a positive user experience, leading to increased user engagement and satisfaction.

14.5 Case Studies: Bootstrap in SPAs

In this section, we'll explore real-world case studies of how Bootstrap can be effectively used in Single Page Applications (SPAs). These examples showcase the versatility and adaptability of Bootstrap in different SPA scenarios.

14.5.1 Case Study 1: Task Management SPA

Scenario: You are building a task management application using React as your SPA framework. Bootstrap is integrated to enhance the application's user interface.

Implementation:

- Bootstrap's responsive grid system is utilized to create a dynamic layout that adapts to various screen sizes.
- Forms and input elements are styled using Bootstrap classes for a clean and intuitive user experience.
- Bootstrap's modal component is employed to create task creation and editing dialogs, providing a consistent and visually appealing interface.
- Tooltips are used for providing additional information when users hover over task items.

```
import React, { useState } from 'react';

import { Button, Modal, Form, Tooltip } from 'react-bootstrap';

function TaskManagementApp() {

const [tasks, setTasks] = useState([]);

const [showModal, setShowModal] = useState(false);

const [taskName, setTaskName] = useState('');

const [taskDescription, setTaskDescription] = useState('');
```

```
const addTask = () => {

const newTask = {

name: taskName,

description: taskDescription,

};

setTasks([...tasks, newTask]);

setShowModal(false);

};

return (

<div>

<h1>Task Management App</h1>

<Button onClick={() => setShowModal(true)}>Add Task</Button>

{tasks.map((task, index) => (

<div key={index} className="task">

<h3>{task.name}</h3>

<p>

<Tooltip title="Task Description" placement="right">

{task.description}

</Tooltip>

</p>
```

```
</div>
))}
<Modal show={showModal} onHide={() => setShowModal(false)}>
<Modal.Header closeButton>
<Modal.Title>Add Task</Modal.Title>
</Modal.Header>
<Modal.Body>
<Form>
<Form.Group controlId="taskName">
<Form.Label>Task Name</Form.Label>
<Form.Control
type="text"
placeholder="Enter task name"
value={taskName}
onChange={(e) => setTaskName(e.target.value)}
/>
</Form.Group>
<Form.Group controlId="taskDescription">
<Form.Label>Task Description</Form.Label>
<Form.Control
```

```
as="textarea"

rows={3}

placeholder="Enter task description"

value={taskDescription}

onChange={(e) => setTaskDescription(e.target.value)}

/>

</Form.Group>

</Form>

</Modal.Body>

<Modal.Footer>

<Button variant="secondary" onClick={() =>
setShowModal(false)}>

Close

</Button>

<Button variant="primary" onClick={addTask}>

Save Task

</Button>

</Modal.Footer>

</Modal>

</div>

);
```

```
}

export default TaskManagementApp;
```

14.5.2 Case Study 2: E-commerce SPA

Scenario: You are developing an e-commerce SPA using Vue.js as your framework. Bootstrap is incorporated to enhance the design and responsiveness of the application.

Implementation:

- Bootstrap's responsive grid system ensures that product listings and shopping cart views adapt to different screen sizes.
- Navigation menus and breadcrumbs are created using Bootstrap's navigation components.
- Bootstrap's modal component is used for displaying product details and allowing users to add items to the cart.
- Responsive images with srcset attributes are employed to serve optimized product images for different devices.

```
<template>

<div>

<h1>E-commerce Store</h1>

<ProductList :products="products" @addToCart="addToCart" />

<ShoppingCart :cart="cart" />

</div>
```

```
</template>
<script>
import ProductList from './ProductList.vue';
import ShoppingCart from './ShoppingCart.vue';
export default {
data() {
return {
products: [
// Product data here...
],
cart: [],
};
},
methods: {
addToCart(product) {
this.cart.push(product);
},
},
components: {
ProductList,
```

```
ShoppingCart,
},
};
</script>
<style scoped>
/* Bootstrap classes can be applied for styling */
</style>
```

14.5.3 Case Study 3: Knowledge Sharing SPA

Scenario: You are creating a knowledge sharing SPA using Angular as your framework. Bootstrap is integrated to provide a user-friendly and consistent design for articles and user profiles.

Implementation:

- Bootstrap's card component is used to display articles with titles, summaries, and publication dates.
- User profiles are designed using Bootstrap's card and layout classes.
- Buttons and forms are styled with Bootstrap for a polished and intuitive user experience.
- Bootstrap's modal component is employed for user authentication and article creation.

```
<div class="container">
<h1>Knowledge Sharing Platform</h1>
```

<div

15.1 Planning and Wireframing

Planning and wireframing are essential steps in the process of building a corporate website using Bootstrap. Before diving into the development phase, it's crucial to establish a clear vision of your website's structure, layout, and content organization. In this section, we'll explore the significance of planning and wireframing in the context of Bootstrap web development.

The Importance of Planning

1. Defining Goals: Start by identifying the primary goals and objectives of your corporate website. What message do you want to convey? Who is your target audience? What actions do you want visitors to take? Clearly defining your goals will guide the entire development process.

2. Content Strategy: Plan your website's content strategically. Determine what information is most important for your audience. Create a content hierarchy that highlights key messages and features. Consider how Bootstrap components can help structure and present your content effectively.

3. User Experience (UX): Think about the overall user experience. How will visitors navigate your site? What should the user journey look like? Sketch out user flows and interactions, keeping in mind Bootstrap's responsive design principles for a seamless experience across devices.

4. Design and Branding: Establish a consistent design and

branding strategy. Choose a color palette, typography, and visual elements that align with your corporate identity. Bootstrap provides customization options to match your brand's look and feel.

Wireframing with Bootstrap

Once you have a clear plan in place, wireframing becomes the next crucial step. Wireframes are simplified, visual representations of your website's layout and structure. Bootstrap can be a valuable tool for creating wireframes:

1. Grid System: Bootstrap's grid system allows you to define the layout of your pages. Use it to create wireframe grids that represent the placement of various elements such as headers, navigation menus, content sections, and footers.

2. Component Placement: Identify the Bootstrap components you intend to use, such as navigation bars, cards, forms, and buttons. Sketch their placement within the wireframe to visualize the overall page structure.

3. Responsive Design: Bootstrap's responsive classes and utilities enable you to plan for different screen sizes. Ensure that your wireframes reflect how the layout will adapt on desktops, tablets, and mobile devices.

4. Content Mockup: While wireframes focus on layout and structure, you can include placeholder content to represent actual text and images. This gives stakeholders a better understanding of the final result.

5. Iterative Process: Wireframing is an iterative process. Share

your wireframes with team members and stakeholders for feedback. Use Bootstrap's flexibility to make adjustments as needed.

```
<!—Example wireframe using Bootstrap classes—>

<div class="container">

<header>

<nav class="navbar navbar-expand-lg navbar-light bg-light">

<!—Navbar content—>

</nav>

</header>

<main>

<div class="row">

<div class="col-md-8">

<h1>Welcome to Our Company</h1>

<p>Lorem ipsum dolor sit amet, consectetur adipiscing elit.</p>

</div>

<div class="col-md-4">

<h2>Latest News</h2>

<ul>

<li>News 1</li>

<li>News 2</li>
```

```
<li>News 3</li>

</ul>

</div>

</div>

</main>

<footer>

<p>&copy; 2023 Our Company. All rights reserved.</p>

</footer>

</div>
```

Benefits of Wireframing with Bootstrap

1. Efficiency: Bootstrap provides a predefined set of UI components and a responsive grid system, saving time during the wireframing process.

2. Consistency: Using Bootstrap ensures a consistent visual language throughout your wireframes, making it easier for stakeholders to understand the design.

3. Flexibility: Bootstrap allows for easy adjustments as project requirements evolve. You can switch between wireframes and prototypes seamlessly.

4. Collaboration: Wireframes created with Bootstrap are shareable and collaborative. Team members can provide feedback and make suggestions based on the visual representation.

5. Alignment with Development: Since Bootstrap is a popular choice for web development, wireframes created with Bootstrap often closely resemble the final product, reducing the gap between design and development.

In conclusion, planning and wireframing are vital steps in the corporate website development process. Bootstrap's grid system, components, and responsive design features make it a valuable tool for creating wireframes that accurately represent your vision and facilitate effective communication with your team and stakeholders.

15.2 Implementing the Homepage

The homepage is often the first impression visitors have of your corporate website. It should effectively communicate your brand's identity, provide essential information, and guide users toward their intended actions. In this section, we'll focus on implementing the homepage of your corporate website using Bootstrap.

Key Elements of a Homepage

1. Header:

- The header typically contains the website's logo, navigation menu, and any essential contact information.
- Bootstrap's Navbar component is an excellent choice for creating a responsive and visually appealing header. Customize it to match your brand's colors and style.

```
<!—Bootstrap Navbar example—>

<nav class="navbar navbar-expand-lg navbar-light bg-light">

<div class="container">

<a class="navbar-brand" href="#">

<img src="logo.png" alt="Company Logo" />

</a>

<button

class="navbar-toggler"

type="button"
```

```
data-bs-toggle="collapse"
data-bs-target="#navbarNav"
aria-controls="navbarNav"
aria-expanded="false"
aria-label="Toggle navigation"
>
<span class="navbar-toggler-icon"></span>
</button>
<div class="collapse navbar-collapse" id="navbarNav">
<ul class="navbar-nav ml-auto">
<li class="nav-item">
<a class="nav-link" href="#">Home</a>
</li>
<li class="nav-item">
<a class="nav-link" href="#">About</a>
</li>
<li class="nav-item">
<a class="nav-link" href="#">Services</a>
</li>
<li class="nav-item">
```

```
<a class="nav-link" href="#">Contact</a>

</li>

</ul>

</div>

</div>

</nav>
```

2. Hero Section:

- The hero section is a prominent area at the top of the homepage, often featuring a captivating image or video along with a call to action (CTA).
- Bootstrap's Jumbotron component is suitable for creating a hero section. Customize it to include your desired content and styling.

```
<!—Bootstrap Jumbotron example for the hero section—>

<div class="jumbotron jumbotron-fluid">

<div class="container">

<h1 class="display-4">Welcome to Our Company</h1>

<p class="lead">We deliver innovative solutions for your business.</p>

<a class="btn btn-primary btn-lg" href="#" role="button">Learn More</a>

</div>
```

```
</div>
```

3. Features or Services Section:

- Highlight the key features or services your company offers. Use Bootstrap's card components to present information in an organized and visually appealing manner.

```
<!—Bootstrap Card example for features or services—>

<div class="container">

<div class="row">

<div class="col-md-4">

<div class="card">

<img src="feature1.png" class="card-img-top" alt="Feature 1" />

<div class="card-body">

<h5 class="card-title">Feature 1</h5>

<p class="card-text">

Lorem ipsum dolor sit amet, consectetur adipiscing elit.

</p>

</div>

</div>

</div>

<!—Add more feature cards here—>
```

```
</div>

</div>
```

4. Call to Action (CTA):

- Encourage user engagement with a clear and compelling CTA. This can be placed within the hero section or separately on the homepage.
- Bootstrap's buttons and styling classes can help create attention-grabbing CTAs.

5. Testimonials or Partners Section:

- Showcase customer testimonials or partnerships to build trust and credibility.
- Bootstrap's carousel component is a useful tool for creating a rotating display of testimonials or partner logos.

```
<!—Bootstrap Carousel example for testimonials or partners—>

<div id="testimonialCarousel" class="carousel slide" data-bs-ride="carousel">

<div class="carousel-inner">

<div class="carousel-item active">

<p>Client Testimonial 1</p>

<h5>John Doe</h5>

</div>
```

```
<!—Add more testimonial items here—>
</div>
<a
class="carousel-control-prev"
href="#testimonialCarousel"
role="button"
data-bs-slide="prev"
>
<span class="carousel-control-prev-icon"
aria-hidden="true"></span>
<span class="visually-hidden">Previous</span>
</a>
<a
class="carousel-control-next"
href="#testimonialCarousel"
role="button"
data-bs-slide="next"
>
<span class="carousel-control-next-icon"
aria-hidden="true"></span>
<span class="visually-hidden">Next</span>
```

```
</a>

</div>
```

6. Footer:

- The footer typically contains contact information, links to important pages, and copyright information.
- Bootstrap's Footer component can be customized to include these elements.

```
<!—Bootstrap Footer example—>

<footer class="bg-light text-center text-lg-start">

<div class="container p-4">

<div class="row">

<div class="col-lg-6 col-md-12 mb-4 mb-md-0">

<h5 class="text-uppercase">Contact Information</h5>

<!—Add contact information here—>

</div>

<div class="col-lg-6 col-md-12 mb-4 mb-md-0">

<h5 class="text-uppercase">Links</h5>

<!—Add footer links here—>

</div>

</div>
```

```
</div>

<div class="text-center p-3">

<p>&copy; 2023 Your Company. All rights reserved.</p>

</div>

</footer>
```

Responsive Design Considerations

Bootstrap's responsive design features ensure that your homepage looks and functions well on various devices and screen sizes. Test your homepage's responsiveness by resizing your browser window and make necessary adjustments to CSS classes and layouts as needed.

In conclusion, implementing the homepage of your corporate website with Bootstrap involves incorporating key elements such as the header, hero section, features/services section, CTAs, testimonials/partners section, and footer. Bootstrap's components and grid system simplify the process while providing a responsive design that caters to a wide range of devices and screen sizes.

15.3 Designing About, Services, and Contact Pages

The About, Services, and Contact pages are fundamental components of a corporate website. These pages provide valuable information about your company, the services you offer, and a means for visitors to get in touch with you. In this section, we'll delve into the design aspects of these pages using Bootstrap.

About Page

The About page serves as a platform to tell your company's story, showcase its history, mission, and values, and introduce the team. Bootstrap can assist in creating an engaging About page:

1. **Introduction Section:** Use a Bootstrap Jumbotron to create a visually appealing introduction section. Highlight your company's vision and values.

```
<!—Bootstrap Jumbotron for About page introduction—>

<div class="jumbotron jumbotron-fluid">

<div class="container">

<h1 class="display-4">Our Story</h1>

<p class="lead">Discover our journey and values that drive us.</p>

</div>

</div>
```

1. **Team Section:** Bootstrap cards can be employed to introduce team members. Include their names, roles, and brief bios. You can organize these cards in a grid layout for easy navigation.

```
<!—Bootstrap Card for team member on About page—>

<div class="card">

<img src="team-member.jpg" class="card-img-top" alt="Team Member">

<div class="card-body">
```

```
<h5 class="card-title">John Doe</h5>

<p class="card-text">Co-founder & CEO</p>

<p class="card-text">Lorem ipsum dolor sit amet, consectetur adipiscing elit.</p>

</div>

</div>
```

1. **History Timeline:** If relevant, create a Bootstrap timeline to showcase the company's history and milestones. This can be a visually appealing way to present your journey.

```
<!—Bootstrap Timeline for About page history— >

<ul class="timeline">

<li>

<div class="timeline-badge">2000</div>

<div class="timeline-panel">

<div class="timeline-heading">

<h4 class="timeline-title">Company Founded</h4>

</div>

<div class="timeline-body">

<p>Lorem ipsum dolor sit amet, consectetur adipiscing elit.</p>

</div>

</div>
```

```
</li>
<!—Add more timeline items here—>
</ul>
```

Services Page

The Services page provides detailed information about the range of services your company offers. Bootstrap can help structure and style this page effectively:

1. **Service Cards:** Utilize Bootstrap cards to present individual services. Include service titles, descriptions, and relevant images.

```
<!—Bootstrap Card for a service on Services page—>
<div class="card">
<img src="service-image.jpg" class="card-img-top" alt="Service Image">
<div class="card-body">
<h5 class="card-title">Web Design</h5>
<p class="card-text">We create stunning and user-friendly websites tailored to your needs.</p>
</div>
</div>
```

1. **Service Categories:** If your services can be grouped into categories, consider using Bootstrap's tabbed navigation to allow users to explore services by category.

```
<!—Bootstrap Tabs for service categories on Services page—>

<ul class="nav nav-tabs" id="serviceTabs" role="tablist">

<li class="nav-item" role="presentation">

<a class="nav-link active" id="category1-tab" data-bs-toggle="tab" href="#category1" role="tab" aria-controls="category1" aria-selected="true">Category 1</a>

</li>

<!—Add more category tabs here—>

</ul>
```

Contact Page

The Contact page is a critical point of interaction between your company and visitors. Bootstrap can facilitate the creation of a user-friendly contact form and other contact details:

1. **Contact Form:** Bootstrap's form components are ideal for designing a contact form. Include fields for name, email, subject, and message. Use the Bootstrap button class for the submission button.

```
<!—Bootstrap Form for contact page—>

<form>

<div class="mb-3">

<label for="name" class="form-label">Name</label>

<input type="text" class="form-control" id="name" placeholder="Your Name">
```

```
</div>

<!—Add more form fields here—>

<button type="submit" class="btn btn-primary">Submit</button>

</form>
```

1. **Contact Details:** Below the form, display your company's contact details, including address, phone number, and email. Bootstrap's typography and layout classes can help structure this information.

```
<!—Bootstrap Contact Details on Contact page—>

<address>

<strong>Company Name</strong><br>

123 Street Name, City<br>

State, ZIP Code<br>

<abbr title="Phone">P:</abbr> (123) 456-7890<br>

<a href="mailto:info@example.com">info@example.com</a>

</address>
```

1. **Map Integration:** If desired, you can integrate a map to show your company's location. Bootstrap can be used to create a container for the map.

```
<!—Bootstrap Map Container on Contact page—>

<div id="map" class="embed-responsive embed-responsive-16by9">
```

```
<!—Map integration code (e.g., Google Maps) goes here—>

</div>
```

In conclusion, designing the About, Services, and Contact pages of your corporate website using Bootstrap allows you to create visually appealing and user-friendly content. Bootstrap's components and styling options streamline the process of presenting essential information about your company, services, and means of contact in a structured and visually appealing manner.

15.4 Adding a Blog Section

A blog section is a valuable addition to your corporate website, offering a platform to share insights, updates, and industry-related content. In this section, we'll explore how to incorporate a blog section into your website using Bootstrap.

Blog Layout

Bootstrap provides a robust grid system and components that can be tailored to create an engaging blog layout:

1. **Blog Cards:** Use Bootstrap cards to present individual blog posts. Each card can contain a featured image, title, publication date, author, and a brief excerpt from the post.

```
<!—Bootstrap Card for a blog post—>

<div class="card mb-3">

<img src="blog-post-image.jpg" class="card-img-top" alt="Blog Post Image">

<div class="card-body">
```

```
<h5 class="card-title">Post Title</h5>

<p class="card-text">Lorem ipsum dolor sit amet, consectetur adipiscing elit.</p>

<p class="card-text"><small class="text-muted">Published on: January 1, 2023</small></p>

</div>

</div>
```

1. **Blog Pagination:** If you have a substantial number of blog posts, consider implementing pagination to allow users to navigate through multiple pages of posts. Bootstrap offers pagination components for this purpose.

```
<!—Bootstrap Pagination for blog posts—>

<ul class="pagination justify-content-center">

<li class="page-item disabled">

<span class="page-link">Previous</span>

</li>

<li class="page-item active" aria-current="page">

<span class="page-link">1</span>

</li>

<!—Add more page links here—>

<li class="page-item">

<a class="page-link" href="#">Next</a>
```

```
</li>

</ul>
```

Blog Post Page

Each blog post should have its dedicated page for in-depth content presentation. Bootstrap can be used to structure these pages effectively:

1. **Single Post Layout:** Use Bootstrap's grid system to create a layout for individual blog post pages. You can have a main content area for the post and a sidebar for additional information or related posts.

```
<!—Bootstrap Grid Layout for a single blog post—>

<div class="row">

<div class="col-md-8">

<!—Main content of the blog post—>

</div>

<div class="col-md-4">

<!—Sidebar with additional information or related posts—>

</div>

</div>
```

1. **Blog Post Content:** Within the main content area, use Bootstrap's typography and styling classes to format your blog post content. You can include headings, paragraphs, images, and links as needed.

```
<!—Bootstrap Typography for blog post content—>

<h1>Blog Post Title</h1>

<p>Lorem ipsum dolor sit amet, consectetur adipiscing elit...</p>

<img src="blog-post-image.jpg" class="img-fluid" alt="Blog Post Image">

<p>Continue reading <a href="#">here</a>.</p>
```

1. **Comments Section:** If you want to allow comments on your blog posts, consider using Bootstrap's form components for the comment submission form. Additionally, you can use a third-party commenting system and integrate it into your Bootstrap-based design.

Blog Post Categories and Tags

To enhance the organization and discoverability of your blog content, you can implement categories and tags using Bootstrap:

1. **Category Filters:** Bootstrap's buttons and filter functionality can be employed to create category filters. Users can click on a category to view posts specifically related to that category.

```
<!—Bootstrap Category Filters—>

<div class="btn-group" role="group" aria-label="Blog Categories">

<button type="button" class="btn btn-secondary">Category 1</button>

<button type="button" class="btn btn-secondary">Category 2</button>
```

```
<!—Add more category buttons here—>

</div>
```

1. **Tag Cloud:** Bootstrap can help style a tag cloud that displays popular tags associated with your blog posts. Users can click on tags to explore related content.

```
<!—Bootstrap Tag Cloud—>

<div class="d-flex flex-wrap">

<a href="#" class="btn btn-outline-primary m-1">Tag 1</a>

<a href="#" class="btn btn-outline-primary m-1">Tag 2</a>

<!—Add more tag buttons here—>

</div>
```

In conclusion, incorporating a blog section into your corporate website using Bootstrap offers numerous benefits. Bootstrap's grid system, cards, pagination, and styling classes allow you to create an organized and visually appealing blog layout. Individual blog post pages can be structured using Bootstrap's grid system and typography classes. Additionally, you can use Bootstrap for category and tag filtering to enhance content organization and user experience on your blog.

15.5 Deployment and Testing

Once you've designed and built your corporate website using Bootstrap, the next crucial steps involve deploying it to a web server and thoroughly testing it to ensure it functions correctly. In this section, we'll explore the deployment and testing processes, along with some best practices.

Deployment

1. Select a Hosting Provider:

- Choose a reliable hosting provider that suits your website's requirements. Options include shared hosting, virtual private servers (VPS), or cloud hosting services.

2. Domain Registration:

- Register a domain name that reflects your brand. Many hosting providers offer domain registration services, or you can use a separate domain registrar.

3. Upload Files:

- Use FTP (File Transfer Protocol) or a web-based file manager provided by your hosting provider to upload your website's files to the server.

4. Database Setup (if applicable):

- If your website relies on a database (e.g., for dynamic content), configure the database and import your data.

5. Configure DNS:

- Update your domain's DNS (Domain Name System) settings to point to your hosting provider's nameservers. This step may take some time to propagate globally.

6. SSL Certificate (HTTPS):

- Secure your website with an SSL certificate to enable HTTPS. Many hosting providers offer free SSL certificates through Let's Encrypt.

Testing

1. Cross-Browser Compatibility:

- Test your website on various web browsers (e.g., Chrome, Firefox, Safari, Edge) to ensure consistent functionality and appearance.

2. Responsiveness:

- Verify that your website is responsive by testing it on different devices (desktop, tablet, smartphone) and screen sizes.

3. Functionality:

- Thoroughly test all website functionality, including forms, navigation, interactive elements, and any third-party integrations (e.g., social media widgets).

4. Performance:

- Use performance testing tools (e.g., Google PageSpeed Insights, GTmetrix) to analyze and optimize your website's loading speed.

5. SEO Readiness:

- Ensure your website is SEO-friendly by optimizing meta tags, headings, alt attributes for images, and ensuring proper URL structure.

6. Content Review:

- Proofread all content, check for broken links, and ensure that images and media load correctly.

7. Security Audit:

- Implement security measures, such as regularly updating your CMS, plugins, and themes, and enabling security plugins or features provided by your hosting provider.

8. Backup Strategy:

- Set up automated backups of your website to safeguard against data loss. Test the backup and restore process to ensure it works.

9. Load Testing:

- If your website is expected to receive high traffic, perform load testing to assess how it handles concurrent users.

10. Accessibility:

- Validate that your website is accessible to all users, including those with disabilities, by testing with accessibility tools and following WCAG guidelines.

11. Mobile App Integration (if applicable):

- **If** you have a mobile app associated **with** your website, test **the** integration **and** functionality **between the** website **and the** app.

Post-Deployment Checklist

After deploying and testing your corporate website, consider the following post-deployment checklist:

- **Monitoring:** Implement website monitoring to receive alerts about downtime or issues.

- **Regular Backups:** Schedule regular backups and verify their integrity.

- **Content Updates:** Plan for ongoing content updates, blogging, and maintenance.

- **Security Updates:** Stay vigilant for security updates and apply them promptly.

- **Analytics:** Set up website analytics (e.g., Google Analytics) to track user behavior and performance.

- **User Training:** If your website involves multiple administrators or content contributors, provide training on CMS usage and best practices.

By following a comprehensive deployment and testing process and staying proactive with maintenance and updates, you can ensure your corporate website remains functional, secure, and user-friendly, providing a positive experience for visitors and achieving your business objectives.

Chapter 16: Project: Creating a Portfolio Site

16.1 Conceptualizing the Portfolio Design

In this section, we'll dive into the initial stages of creating a portfolio website using Bootstrap. A portfolio site is a powerful tool for showcasing your work, skills, and accomplishments to potential clients or employers. Before we start coding, it's crucial to conceptualize the design and layout of your portfolio.

Define Your Goals and Audience

Before diving into design, consider your goals and target audience. Are you a designer, developer, photographer, or a professional from another field? Knowing your audience will help you tailor your portfolio to their expectations and needs.

Content Planning

Outline the content you want to showcase. This typically includes projects, case studies, a brief bio, resume, and contact information. Make a list of the projects or works you want to feature.

Visual Style

Think about the visual style that represents your brand or personal identity. Choose a color scheme, typography, and imagery that aligns with your message. Bootstrap provides a great starting point with its predefined styles, but you can customize it further.

Layout and Navigation

Consider how you want to organize your content. A typical portfolio includes a homepage, project pages, an about section, and a contact page. Plan the navigation menu and decide if you want a one-page scrolling design or a multi-page layout.

Wireframing

Create rough sketches or wireframes of your portfolio's pages. This helps visualize the layout, placement of elements, and overall flow. Tools like Balsamiq or pen and paper can be handy for this step.

Mobile Responsiveness

Remember that your portfolio should be responsive and look great on various devices. Bootstrap's responsive grid system will come in handy for achieving this. Test your wireframes on different screen sizes.

User Experience

Think about the user experience (UX) you want to provide. Ensure that your portfolio is easy to navigate, loads quickly, and presents your work effectively.

Content Strategy

Develop a content strategy that emphasizes your best work and achievements. Write engaging and concise project descriptions. Consider adding keywords for SEO purposes.

Portfolio Inspiration

Take a look at other portfolios online for inspiration. Note what you like and what you think works well. Use this as a reference, but make sure your portfolio reflects your unique style.

Conclusion

By carefully conceptualizing your portfolio design, you'll have a clear vision of what you want to create. This initial planning phase is crucial for a successful and visually appealing portfolio website.

Now that we have a conceptual plan in place, we can move on to implementing the design using Bootstrap components in the following sections.

16.2 Showcasing Work with Bootstrap Components

In this section, we'll focus on showcasing your work effectively using Bootstrap components. Your portfolio should not only look visually appealing but also provide an engaging and informative experience for visitors. Bootstrap offers various components to help you achieve this.

Portfolio Grid

One of the central elements of a portfolio is the grid that displays your projects or works. Bootstrap's grid system is a perfect choice for creating a responsive and organized portfolio grid. Here's an example of how you can structure your portfolio grid:

```
<div class="container">

<div class="row">
```

```
<div class="col-md-4">

<!—Project 1 content here—>

</div>

<div class="col-md-4">

<!—Project 2 content here—>

</div>

<div class="col-md-4">

<!—Project 3 content here—>

</div>

</div>

</div>
```

You can customize the number of columns and layout according to your preferences. Each project or work can be placed within a col-md-4 or any other suitable column class.

Project Cards

Bootstrap provides card components that are perfect for showcasing individual projects. Here's an example of how you can create a project card:

```
<div class="card">

<img src="project-image.jpg" class="card-img-top" alt="Project Image">

<div class="card-body">
```

```
<h5 class="card-title">Project Title</h5>

<p class="card-text">Project description goes here.</p>

<a href="#" class="btn btn-primary">View Project</a>

</div>

</div>
```

You can customize the card's content, image, and button text to suit your project details. Repeat this structure for each project in your portfolio grid.

Filtering and Sorting

If you have a large number of projects, consider adding filtering and sorting functionality to make it easier for visitors to navigate. You can use JavaScript libraries like Isotope or MixItUp to achieve this. Here's a simplified example using Isotope:

```
<div class="filters">

<button data-filter="*">All</button>

<button data-filter=".web-design">Web Design</button>

<button data-filter=".graphic-design">Graphic Design</button>

</div>

<div class="container">

<div class="row">

<div class="col-md-4 web-design">

<!—Web Design Project Content—>
```

```
</div>

<div class="col-md-4 graphic-design">

<!—Graphic Design Project Content—>

</div>

</div>

</div>
```

You'll need to include Isotope's JavaScript library for this to work fully.

Project Details Pages

For each project in your portfolio, consider creating individual project details pages. These pages can provide in-depth information about the project, including images, descriptions, technologies used, and more. Bootstrap can be used to structure these pages as well.

```
<div class="container">

<div class="row">

<div class="col-md-8">

<h2>Project Title</h2>

<p>Project description and details go here.</p>

<!—Add more content as needed—>

</div>

<div class="col-md-4">

<!—Additional project details, images, or related content—>
```

```
</div>

</div>

</div>
```

Ensure that each project card links to its respective project details page.

Testimonials and Client Feedback

Consider adding a section for client testimonials or feedback to build trust with your visitors. Bootstrap's carousel component can be used to create a rotating testimonial section.

```
<div id="testimonial-carousel" class="carousel slide" data-ride="carousel">

<div class="carousel-inner">

<div class="carousel-item active">

<p>Client feedback or testimonial goes here.</p>

<h5>Client Name</h5>

</div>

<!—Add more testimonials as needed—>

</div>

<a class="carousel-control-prev" href="#testimonial-carousel" role="button" data-slide="prev">

<span class="carousel-control-prev-icon" aria-hidden="true"></span>
```

```
<span class="sr-only">Previous</span>

</a>

<a class="carousel-control-next" href="#testimonial-carousel" role="button" data-slide="next">

<span class="carousel-control-next-icon" aria-hidden="true"></span>

<span class="sr-only">Next</span>

</a>

</div>
```

Customize the testimonials and add more slides as needed.

Conclusion

Effectively showcasing your work using Bootstrap components can make your portfolio stand out. Remember to keep the user experience in mind and provide clear and engaging content for your visitors. In the next section, we'll explore integrating multimedia content to enhance your portfolio further.

16.3 Integrating Multimedia Content

In this section, we'll focus on enhancing your portfolio website by integrating multimedia content. Multimedia elements like images, videos, and interactive features can significantly enrich the user experience and make your portfolio more engaging.

Image Galleries

Adding image galleries to your portfolio is a great way to showcase your visual work. Bootstrap provides a responsive and easy-to-implement Carousel component that's perfect for creating image galleries.

```
<div id="image-gallery" class="carousel slide" data-ride="carousel">

<div class="carousel-inner">

<div class="carousel-item active">

<img src="image1.jpg" class="d-block w-100" alt="Image 1">

</div>

<div class="carousel-item">

<img src="image2.jpg" class="d-block w-100" alt="Image 2">

</div>

<!—Add more images as needed—>

</div>

<a class="carousel-control-prev" href="#image-gallery" role="button" data-slide="prev">

<span class="carousel-control-prev-icon" aria-hidden="true"></span>

<span class="sr-only">Previous</span>

</a>
```

```
<a class="carousel-control-next" href="#image-gallery" role="button" data-slide="next">

<span class="carousel-control-next-icon" aria-hidden="true"></span>

<span class="sr-only">Next</span>

</a>

</div>
```

Customize the image sources and add more items to the carousel for your image gallery.

Video Integration

If you have videos related to your projects or work, you can embed them in your portfolio. You can use the HTML <video> tag to embed videos and make them responsive with Bootstrap.

```
<video controls class="embed-responsive embed-responsive-16by9">

<source src="video.mp4" type="video/mp4">

Your browser does not support the video tag.

</video>
```

Ensure you provide multiple video formats for cross-browser compatibility (e.g., MP4, WebM, Ogg). The embed-responsive class ensures the video scales appropriately.

Interactive Features

Consider adding interactive features to engage your visitors further. Bootstrap components like modals, tooltips, and popovers can be used to create interactive elements.

```
<button type="button" class="btn btn-primary" data-toggle="modal" data-target="#myModal">

Launch Modal

</button>

<div class="modal fade" id="myModal">

<div class="modal-dialog">

<div class="modal-content">

<!—Modal content goes here—>

</div>

</div>

</div>
```

Modals can be used to display additional project details, case studies, or interactive content.

Embedding Code Snippets

If you're a developer, consider showcasing your code snippets within your portfolio. You can use HTML <code> and <pre> tags to display code blocks with syntax highlighting libraries like Prism or highlight.js for a more visually appealing presentation.

```
<pre>
```

```
<code class="language-javascript">

// Your code here

</code>

</pre>
```

Conclusion

Integrating multimedia content into your portfolio can make it more dynamic and engaging. Whether it's showcasing images, videos, or interactive elements, Bootstrap provides the flexibility and tools to make your portfolio visually appealing and interactive. In the next section, we'll explore ways to enhance the overall user experience and optimize your portfolio for search engines.

16.4 Enhancing User Experience

In this section, we'll delve into techniques to enhance the user experience (UX) of your portfolio website. A positive UX can leave a lasting impression on your visitors and make them more likely to engage with your content and services.

Responsive Design

Ensuring your portfolio is responsive is essential for providing a seamless experience across various devices and screen sizes. Bootstrap's responsive grid system makes it easier to create layouts that adapt to different screen resolutions.

```
<div class="container">

<div class="row">

<div class="col-lg-6 col-md-12">
```

```
<!—Content for large screens—>

</div>

<div class="col-lg-6 col-md-12">

<!—Content for large screens—>

</div>

</div>

</div>
```

By specifying different column classes for different screen sizes (e.g., col-lg-6 for large screens and col-md-12 for medium screens), you can control how your content is displayed.

Smooth Navigation

Ensure that your navigation menu is user-friendly and intuitive. Bootstrap provides a Navbar component that can be used to create a responsive and collapsible navigation menu.

```
<nav class="navbar navbar-expand-lg navbar-light bg-light">

<a class="navbar-brand" href="#">Portfolio</a>

<button class="navbar-toggler" type="button" data-toggle="collapse" data-target="#navbarNav" aria-controls="navbarNav" aria-expanded="false" aria-label="Toggle navigation">

<span class="navbar-toggler-icon"></span>

</button>

<div class="collapse navbar-collapse" id="navbarNav">
```

```
<ul class="navbar-nav">

<li class="nav-item active">

<a class="nav-link" href="#section1">Home</a>

</li>

<li class="nav-item">

<a class="nav-link" href="#section2">Projects</a>

</li>

<li class="nav-item">

<a class="nav-link" href="#section3">About</a>

</li>

<li class="nav-item">

<a class="nav-link" href="#section4">Contact</a>

</li>

</ul>

</div>

</nav>
```

The collapsible navigation menu is particularly useful for mobile users, making it easier for them to access different sections of your portfolio.

Performance Optimization

Optimizing your portfolio's performance is crucial for a smooth user experience. Compress images, minify CSS and JavaScript, and leverage browser caching to reduce load times. Bootstrap's built-in optimizations can help, but you should also consider using a content delivery network (CDN) and server-side optimizations.

Accessibility

Make sure your portfolio is accessible to all users, including those with disabilities. Bootstrap includes features for accessible components, but you should also follow best practices for web accessibility, such as providing alternative text for images and using semantic HTML elements.

SEO Optimization

Optimize your portfolio for search engines (SEO) to improve its visibility in search results. Use descriptive titles and meta descriptions, include relevant keywords, and create clean and organized HTML structures. Consider using schema markup to provide structured data to search engines.

User Testing

Before launching your portfolio, conduct user testing to identify any usability issues or areas for improvement. Gather feedback from friends, colleagues, or potential users to refine your portfolio's user experience.

Feedback and Contact

Include a contact form or contact information on your portfolio, allowing visitors to reach out to you easily. Encourage feedback and inquiries to build a connection with your audience.

Conclusion

Enhancing the user experience of your portfolio is essential for making a lasting impression on your visitors. By focusing on responsive design, smooth navigation, performance optimization, accessibility, SEO, user testing, and engagement through feedback, you can create a portfolio that effectively showcases your work and skills while providing an excellent user experience. In the next section, we'll explore the importance of SEO and analytics for tracking your portfolio's performance.

16.5 SEO and Analytics

In this section, we'll discuss the importance of Search Engine Optimization (SEO) and analytics for your portfolio website. SEO helps your website rank higher in search engine results, making it more discoverable, while analytics allow you to track user behavior and make data-driven decisions for improvement.

Search Engine Optimization (SEO)

Optimizing your portfolio for search engines is crucial for increasing its visibility. Here are some key SEO practices to implement:

1. **Keyword Research**: Identify relevant keywords and phrases related to your work and industry. Use tools like Google Keyword Planner or SEMrush to find suitable keywords.

2. **On-Page Optimization**: Ensure that your portfolio pages have descriptive titles, meta descriptions, and headings that incorporate your target keywords. Use semantic HTML5 elements to structure your content properly.
3. **Image Optimization**: Add descriptive alt text to images. Compress images to reduce page load times while maintaining image quality.
4. **Content Quality**: Create high-quality, informative, and engaging content. This can include detailed project descriptions, blog posts, or case studies related to your work.
5. **Mobile-Friendliness**: Ensure that your portfolio is responsive and looks great on mobile devices. Google prioritizes mobile-friendly websites in search results.
6. **Page Speed**: Optimize your website's performance by minimizing CSS and JavaScript files, leveraging browser caching, and using a content delivery network (CDN).
7. **Backlinks**: Build high-quality backlinks to your portfolio by guest posting on relevant blogs, sharing your work on social media, and participating in industry forums.
8. **Sitemap and Robots.txt**: Create a sitemap.xml file to help search engines crawl your website efficiently. Use a robots.txt file to control which parts of your site should not be indexed.

Analytics

Analytics tools provide valuable insights into how users interact with your portfolio. Google Analytics is a popular choice for tracking website performance. Here's how to set it up:

1. **Create a Google Analytics Account**: Visit the Google Analytics website, sign in with your Google account, and

create a new analytics property for your portfolio website.

2. **Install the Tracking Code**: Google Analytics provides a tracking code snippet that you need to add to every page of your website, typically just before the closing </head> tag.

```
<!—Google Analytics Tracking Code—>

<script async src="https://www.googletagmanager.com/gtag/js?id=YOUR_GA_TRACKING_ID"></script>

<script>

window.dataLayer = window.dataLayer || [];

function gtag() {

dataLayer.push(arguments);

}

gtag('js', new Date());

gtag('config', 'YOUR_GA_TRACKING_ID');

</script>
```

Replace YOUR_GA_TRACKING_ID with your actual Google Analytics tracking ID.

1. **Set Up Goals**: Define goals in Google Analytics, such as tracking contact form submissions or clicks on specific links. Goals help you measure the effectiveness of your website.
2. **Analyze Data**: Use Google Analytics to monitor website traffic, user behavior, demographics, and more. Analyze this data to identify areas for improvement and track the

success of your portfolio.

3. **Regular Reporting**: Set up regular reports to receive insights via email. This can help you stay informed about your website's performance without needing to log in regularly.

SEO and Analytics Plugins

If you're using a content management system like WordPress, you can find SEO and analytics plugins to simplify the implementation of these practices. Popular SEO plugins include Yoast SEO and All in One SEO Pack, while Google Analytics can be easily integrated with plugins or added using Google Tag Manager.

Conclusion

Implementing SEO best practices and using analytics tools like Google Analytics are essential steps to ensure that your portfolio website is both discoverable and effectively meeting your goals. These tools provide valuable data and insights that can help you continually improve your portfolio's performance and user experience.

Chapter 17: Project: Developing an Educational Platform

17.1 Structuring Course Content

In this section, we will embark on the journey of developing an educational platform as part of your portfolio. An educational platform can be a powerful showcase of your web development skills while also serving as a valuable resource for learners. Before diving into the technical aspects, it's essential to structure the course content effectively.

Define Your Course Topics

Begin by defining the topics or subjects you want to cover in your educational platform. Whether it's coding tutorials, language learning, or any other field, a clear understanding of your course's content is crucial.

Course Outline

Create a course outline or syllabus that outlines the modules, lessons, and topics you plan to cover. Each module should have a clear objective and learning outcomes.

Organize Content Hierarchically

Structure your content hierarchically. You can use headings and subheadings to break down your modules and lessons. For example:

- Module 1: Introduction to Web Development

- Lesson 1: What is HTML?

- Lesson 2: HTML Tags and Elements

- Lesson 3: Creating Your First Web Page

- Module 2: CSS Styling

- Lesson 1: Introduction to CSS

- Lesson 2: CSS Selectors and Properties

- Lesson 3: Styling Web Pages with CSS

Multimedia Integration

Consider how you can integrate multimedia elements into your course content. This might include video tutorials, interactive quizzes, and downloadable resources like PDFs or code examples.

Consistent Navigation

Ensure that your educational platform has a consistent and intuitive navigation structure. Users should be able to easily move between modules, lessons, and other course components.

User Registration

If you plan to allow user registration for tracking progress or providing certificates, design a user registration system. Bootstrap can help you create user-friendly forms for registration and login.

Responsive Design

Make sure your educational platform is responsive, as learners might access it from various devices. Bootstrap's responsive grid system will be handy for achieving this.

Accessibility

Follow web accessibility guidelines to ensure that your content is accessible to all users, including those with disabilities. This is especially important for educational platforms.

Interactive Features

Consider adding interactive features such as quizzes, assignments, or discussion forums to engage learners and encourage active participation.

Content Management

Think about how you will manage and update course content over time. A content management system (CMS) can be helpful for easily adding, editing, and organizing lessons and modules.

Conclusion

Structuring your course content effectively is the foundation of creating a successful educational platform. With a clear organization, user-friendly navigation, multimedia integration, and attention to accessibility, you can provide an engaging and valuable learning experience for your users. In the next section, we'll explore interactive features and user engagement for your educational platform.

17.2 Interactive Features for Learning

In this section, we'll delve into the creation of interactive features to enhance the learning experience on your educational platform. Interactive elements can make the learning process more engaging and effective for your users.

Interactive Quizzes

One effective way to engage learners is by incorporating interactive quizzes into your course content. Bootstrap can help you create user-friendly quiz forms with its form components.

```
<form>

<div class="form-group">

<label for="question1">Question 1: What is HTML?</label>

<input type="text" class="form-control" id="question1" name="question1">

</div>

<div class="form-group">

<label for="question2">Question 2: What does CSS stand for?</label>

<select class="form-control" id="question2" name="question2">

<option value="select">Select an option</option>

<option value="cascading">Cascading Style Sheets</option>

<option value="correct">Correct Style Syntax</option>

<option value="computer">Computer Style System</option>

</select>

</div>

<!—Add more quiz questions here—>
```

```
<button type="submit" class="btn btn-primary">Submit Quiz</button>

</form>
```

You can extend this form for more complex quizzes and handle user responses with server-side scripting or JavaScript.

Interactive Assignments

If your course includes assignments or coding exercises, create a dedicated section for learners to complete and submit their work. You can use Bootstrap forms for assignment submissions and provide clear instructions.

```
<form>

<div class="form-group">

<label for="assignmentTitle">Assignment Title</label>

<input type="text" class="form-control" id="assignmentTitle" name="assignmentTitle">

</div>

<div class="form-group">

<label for="assignmentDescription">Assignment Description</label>

<textarea class="form-control" id="assignmentDescription" name="assignmentDescription" rows="4"></textarea>

</div>

<!—Add file upload or code input fields as needed—>
```

```
<button type="submit" class="btn btn-primary">Submit Assignment</button>

</form>
```

Ensure that you have a system to review and provide feedback on submitted assignments.

Discussion Forums

Implementing a discussion forum where learners can ask questions, share insights, and interact with fellow students can foster a sense of community. You can use Bootstrap to create a clean and organized forum layout.

```
<div class="container">

<h2>Discussion Forum</h2>

<div class="row">

<div class="col-md-8">

<!—Forum posts and discussions go here—>

</div>

<div class="col-md-4">

<!—Sidebar with categories or recent posts—>

</div>

</div>

</div>
```

Consider integrating third-party forum software or using JavaScript frameworks for real-time interactions.

Progress Tracking

Implement a progress tracking system that allows learners to see their course progress and achievements. Bootstrap's progress bars or badges can be used for this purpose.

```
<div class="progress">

<div class="progress-bar" role="progressbar" style="width: 75%;" aria-valuenow="75" aria-valuemin="0" aria-valuemax="100">

75%

</div>

</div>
```

Update the progress bar dynamically based on a learner's completion of modules or quizzes.

Gamification

Consider adding gamification elements such as badges, certificates, or leaderboards to motivate learners and reward their progress and achievements.

User Interaction Feedback

Collect feedback from learners to understand their needs and improve the learning experience continuously. Bootstrap can be used to create feedback forms or surveys.

Conclusion

By incorporating interactive features like quizzes, assignments, discussion forums, progress tracking, and gamification, you can create a dynamic and engaging learning experience on your educational platform. These elements can foster a sense of community among learners and enhance their understanding of the course material. In the next section, we'll focus on user registration and building a user dashboard for your educational platform.

17.3 User Registration and Dashboard

In this section, we'll explore the process of implementing user registration and building a user dashboard for your educational platform. User registration allows learners to create accounts, track their progress, and access course materials more conveniently.

User Registration Form

Begin by designing a user-friendly registration form that captures essential information from users. Bootstrap's form components can help you create an organized and visually appealing registration form.

```
<form>

<div class="form-group">

<label for="fullName">Full Name</label>

<input type="text" class="form-control" id="fullName" name="fullName">

</div>

<div class="form-group">
```

```
<label for="email">Email Address</label>

<input type="email" class="form-control" id="email" name="email">

</div>

<div class="form-group">

<label for="password">Password</label>

<input type="password" class="form-control" id="password" name="password">

</div>

<!—Add more fields as needed—>

<button type="submit" class="btn btn-primary">Register</button>

</form>
```

Ensure that you validate user input, store passwords securely (hashed and salted), and implement necessary security measures to protect user data.

User Authentication

Implement user authentication to allow registered users to log in. Bootstrap can help you design a clean and user-friendly login form.

```
<form>

<div class="form-group">

<label for="loginEmail">Email Address</label>
```

```
<input type="email" class="form-control" id="loginEmail" name="loginEmail">

</div>

<div class="form-group">

<label for="loginPassword">Password</label>

<input type="password" class="form-control" id="loginPassword" name="loginPassword">

</div>

<button type="submit" class="btn btn-primary">Log In</button>

</form>
```

Utilize server-side authentication libraries or frameworks to manage user sessions securely.

User Dashboard

Create a user dashboard where learners can access course materials, view their progress, and interact with course components. Bootstrap's responsive grid system can help structure the dashboard layout effectively.

```
<div class="container">

<h2>User Dashboard</h2>

<div class="row">

<div class="col-md-3">

<!—Sidebar with user profile and navigation—>
```

```
</div>

<div class="col-md-9">

<!—Main content area with course modules, progress, and interactions—>

</div>

</div>

</div>
```

The dashboard can include sections for course modules, progress tracking, interactive quizzes, assignments, and discussion forums.

Progress Tracking

Display the learner's progress within the dashboard. You can use Bootstrap's progress bars to visualize progress on individual modules or lessons.

```
<div class="progress">

<div class="progress-bar" role="progressbar" style="width: 75%;" aria-valuenow="75" aria-valuemin="0" aria-valuemax="100">

75%

</div>

</div>
```

Update the progress dynamically as learners complete lessons or quizzes.

Interactive Components

Integrate interactive components within the dashboard, such as buttons to start courses, links to access modules, and notifications for achievements or course updates.

User Profile

Allow users to update their profiles, change passwords, and manage account settings within the dashboard.

Conclusion

Implementing user registration and creating a user dashboard is essential for providing learners with a personalized and convenient learning experience on your educational platform. Bootstrap's design components can help you create visually appealing and user-friendly registration forms, login forms, and dashboards. In the next section, we'll focus on integrating multimedia content into your educational platform to enhance the learning experience further.

17.4 Integrating Video and Media

In this section, we'll explore the integration of video and multimedia content into your educational platform. Video lectures, tutorials, and multimedia resources can significantly enhance the learning experience and make your platform more engaging.

Video Lectures

Consider creating video lectures to explain complex concepts or demonstrate practical tasks. You can use popular video hosting platforms like YouTube or Vimeo to host your videos. Embedding videos in your educational platform is straightforward.

```
<iframe width="560" height="315" src="https://www.youtube.com/embed/YOUR_VIDEO_ID" frameborder="0" allowfullscreen></iframe>
```

Replace YOUR_VIDEO_ID with the actual ID of your video. You can customize the width and height as needed to fit your platform's design.

Interactive Multimedia

Enhance your course materials with interactive multimedia elements like interactive simulations, 3D models, or virtual labs. Depending on the complexity, you might need to use third-party libraries or frameworks to implement these features effectively.

```
<!—Example: Embedding an interactive simulation using an iframe—>
```

```
<iframe src="https://example.com/simulation" width="800" height="600"></iframe>
```

Ensure that interactive elements are responsive and work seamlessly on various devices.

Document Resources

Provide downloadable resources such as PDFs, eBooks, or slideshows to supplement your course materials. Bootstrap's buttons and links can be used to offer easy access to these resources.

```
<a href="your_resource.pdf" class="btn btn-primary" download>Download PDF</a>
```

The download attribute ensures that the file is downloaded when clicked.

Multimedia Accessibility

Pay attention to accessibility when integrating multimedia content. Provide captions and transcripts for videos to make them accessible to users with disabilities. Ensure that interactive multimedia elements are keyboard navigable and have alternative text where applicable.

Multimedia Hosting and Bandwidth

Consider the hosting and bandwidth requirements for multimedia content. Depending on your platform's traffic and the size of your multimedia files, you may need a reliable hosting solution with sufficient bandwidth to deliver content smoothly.

Responsive Design

Ensure that multimedia content is responsive and adjusts to different screen sizes. Bootstrap's responsive design principles can help maintain a consistent user experience on various devices.

User Engagement

Encourage user engagement with multimedia content by incorporating interactive elements such as quizzes, polls, or discussions related to the content.

Copyright and Licensing

Respect copyright laws and licensing agreements when using multimedia content. If you're creating your own videos or multimedia resources, consider licensing them under Creative Commons or similar licenses to allow for wider sharing and use.

Testing and Quality

Regularly test multimedia elements to ensure they function correctly and provide a high-quality experience. Consider user feedback to improve the quality and relevance of multimedia resources.

Conclusion

Integrating video lectures, interactive multimedia, and downloadable resources into your educational platform can greatly enrich the learning experience. Whether you're explaining complex concepts through videos or providing interactive simulations, Bootstrap's responsive design capabilities can help ensure a consistent and accessible multimedia experience for your learners. In the next section, we'll explore the importance of a secure and scalable architecture for your educational platform.

17.5 Secure and Scalable Architecture

In this section, we'll discuss the significance of implementing a secure and scalable architecture for your educational platform. A robust architecture ensures that your platform can handle growing user numbers and provides a safe environment for user data.

Secure User Data

Security should be a top priority when developing your platform. Ensure that user data, including personal information and login credentials, is stored securely. Use encryption to protect sensitive data in transit and at rest.

```
// Example: Encrypting user passwords before storage

const bcrypt = require('bcrypt');
```

```
const plaintextPassword = 'user_password';

const saltRounds = 10;

bcrypt.hash(plaintextPassword, saltRounds, function(err, hash) {

// Store 'hash' in your database

});
```

Implement security best practices such as password hashing and salting to protect user passwords.

Authentication and Authorization

Implement robust authentication and authorization mechanisms to ensure that only authorized users can access certain parts of your platform. Use token-based authentication or session management, depending on your architecture.

```
// Example: Using JSON Web Tokens (JWT) for authentication

const jwt = require('jsonwebtoken');

const user = { id: 1, username: 'user@example.com' };

const secretKey = 'your_secret_key';

const token = jwt.sign(user, secretKey);
```

Authorization controls what actions users are allowed to perform within your platform. Ensure that users can only access the content and features they are authorized for.

Secure APIs

If your platform includes APIs for interactions such as submitting assignments or accessing course materials, secure them using API keys, OAuth, or other authentication methods. Implement rate limiting and access controls to prevent abuse.

```
// Example: Securing an API endpoint with an API key
const apiKey = 'your_api_key';
app.get('/api/resource', (req, res) => {
const providedApiKey = req.headers['api-key'];
if (providedApiKey === apiKey) {
// Return the resource
} else {
// Unauthorized access
res.status(401).send('Unauthorized');
}
});
```

Scalability

Plan for scalability from the beginning. As your user base grows, your platform should be able to handle increased traffic. Consider cloud-based hosting solutions that can scale automatically to meet demand.

```
// Example: Using AWS Elastic Beanstalk for scalable hosting
// (Note: This is just one of many options)
```

Content Delivery Network (CDN)

Utilize a Content Delivery Network (CDN) to distribute multimedia content efficiently. CDNs help reduce server load and improve content delivery speed by caching and serving content from geographically distributed servers.

```
<!—Example: Adding a CDN link for Bootstrap CSS—>

<link

rel="stylesheet"

href="https://stackpath.bootstrapcdn.com/bootstrap/4.5.2/css/
bootstrap.min.css"

integrity="sha384-pzjw8f+ua6Zl5F5r5sktJw6Hb6z9YJ5f6tzu6s9J6vGorw
crossorigin="anonymous"

>
```

Regular Security Audits

Perform regular security audits and vulnerability assessments to identify and mitigate potential security risks. Stay updated with security patches and best practices to protect your platform.

Compliance and Regulations

Depending on your audience and location, you may need to comply with data protection regulations such as GDPR or COPPA. Familiarize yourself with relevant legal requirements and ensure that your platform adheres to them.

Disaster Recovery

Have a disaster recovery plan in place to handle unexpected events such as server failures or data breaches. Regularly backup user data and have a plan for restoring services quickly.

Conclusion

A secure and scalable architecture is vital for the success and longevity of your educational platform. By focusing on data security, user authentication, API security, scalability, CDN usage, security audits, compliance, and disaster recovery, you can create a platform that provides a safe and reliable learning environment for your users. In the next chapter, we'll explore the importance of web accessibility and considerations for a global audience.

Chapter 18: Accessibility and Internationalization

18.1 Ensuring Web Accessibility

In this section, we'll emphasize the importance of web accessibility for your educational platform. Web accessibility ensures that your platform is usable by individuals with disabilities and provides a seamless experience for all users.

What Is Web Accessibility?

Web accessibility means designing and developing your platform in a way that people with disabilities can perceive, understand, navigate, and interact with it effectively. Disabilities that may affect web users include visual, auditory, cognitive, motor, and speech impairments.

Why Web Accessibility Matters

1. **Inclusivity**: Web accessibility ensures that everyone, regardless of their abilities, can access and benefit from your educational content. It promotes inclusivity and equal opportunities for learning.
2. **Legal Requirements**: Many countries have laws and regulations that require websites and educational platforms to be accessible. Non-compliance can lead to legal consequences.
3. **Enhanced User Experience**: Accessibility improvements often lead to better overall user experiences, benefiting all users, not just those with disabilities.

Web Accessibility Guidelines

To ensure web accessibility, you should follow established guidelines and standards. The Web Content Accessibility Guidelines (WCAG) are the most widely recognized and provide detailed criteria for accessibility.

<!—Example: Adding an alt attribute for images for screen readers—>

<img src="image.jpg" **alt**="A student studying with a laptop">

WCAG covers areas like text alternatives for non-text content, keyboard accessibility, time-based media, adaptable content, and more.

Screen Readers and Assistive Technologies

Ensure that your platform is compatible with screen readers and assistive technologies like voice recognition software. Test your platform using screen readers to identify and fix issues.

Semantic HTML

Use semantic HTML elements (e.g., <header>, <nav>, <main>, <footer>) to structure your content properly. Semantic elements help screen readers and search engines understand the content's hierarchy.

<!—Example: Using semantic HTML elements for page structure—>

<header>

<h1>Course Title**</h1>**

<nav>

```
<ul>

<li><a href="#overview">Overview</a></li>

<li><a href="#lessons">Lessons</a></li>

</ul>

</nav>

</header>
```

Keyboard Navigation

Ensure that all interactive elements, links, and forms can be accessed and used with a keyboard. Keyboard navigation is essential for users who cannot use a mouse.

```
<!—Example: Adding keyboard focus styles for interactive elements—>

<button class="btn btn-primary" tabindex="0">Click me</button>
```

Testing and Validation

Regularly test your platform for accessibility using automated tools and manual testing with assistive technologies. Address and fix accessibility issues as they arise.

Conclusion

Web accessibility is a fundamental aspect of creating an inclusive and user-friendly educational platform. By adhering to accessibility guidelines, using semantic HTML, ensuring keyboard navigation, and regularly testing your platform, you can make learning accessible to a wider audience. In the next section, we'll delve into multilingual support and considerations for catering to a global audience.

18.2 Multilingual Support in Bootstrap

In this section, we'll explore how to implement multilingual support in your Bootstrap-based educational platform. Offering content in multiple languages can significantly expand your audience and cater to learners from diverse linguistic backgrounds.

Language Selection

The first step in providing multilingual support is to allow users to select their preferred language. You can create a language dropdown or menu in your platform's header or settings.

```
<!—Example: Language selection dropdown—>

<div class="dropdown">

<button class="btn btn-secondary dropdown-toggle" type="button" id="languageDropdown" data-toggle="dropdown" aria-haspopup="true" aria-expanded="false">

Language

</button>

<div class="dropdown-menu" aria-labelledby="languageDropdown">

<a class="dropdown-item" href="?lang=en">English</a>

<a class="dropdown-item" href="?lang=es">Español</a>

<!—Add more language options—>
```

```
</div>

</div>
```

Each language option should have a unique identifier, such as "en" for English and "es" for Spanish.

Localization Files

Bootstrap itself does not include multilingual support out of the box, but you can create localization (l10n) files for your content. These files contain translations of all text elements used in your platform.

```
// Example: Localization file for English

{

"welcome_message": "Welcome to our educational platform!",

"learn_more": "Learn More",

"contact_us": "Contact Us"

}
```

For each supported language, create a corresponding localization file.

Dynamic Content Loading

When a user selects a language, load the corresponding localization file and replace the content on your platform dynamically. JavaScript can help you achieve this.

```
// Example: Dynamic content loading based on selected language

const selectedLanguage = 'en'; // Retrieve this from the user's selection
```

```
fetch(`localization/${selectedLanguage}.json`)

.then(response => response.json())

.then(data => {

document.querySelector('.welcome-message').textContent = data.welcome_message;

document.querySelector('.learn-more').textContent = data.learn_more;

document.querySelector('.contact-us').textContent = data.contact_us;

// Update other elements as needed

});
```

RTL Languages

If you support languages that are written right-to-left (RTL), ensure that your platform's layout and styles accommodate RTL text direction. Bootstrap provides classes like text-right and dir="rtl" to help with RTL support.

SEO Considerations

Consider the impact of multilingual content on search engine optimization (SEO). Implement hreflang tags to inform search engines about language and regional targeting.

```
<!—Example: hreflang tags for multilingual content—>

<link rel="alternate" hreflang="en" href="https://example.com/en/page">
```

```html
<link rel="alternate" hreflang="es" href="https://example.com/es/página">

<!--Add tags for other supported languages-->
```

User-Generated Content

If your platform allows user-generated content, such as forum posts or comments, support multilingual input and consider implementing moderation to ensure content quality.

Conclusion

Implementing multilingual support in your Bootstrap-based educational platform can open up new opportunities to reach a global audience. By providing language selection options, creating localization files, dynamically loading content, accommodating RTL languages, and considering SEO and user-generated content, you can create a welcoming and accessible platform for learners from around the world. In the next section, we'll delve into cultural considerations in design for a diverse user base.

18.3 Cultural Considerations in Design

In this section, we'll explore the importance of cultural considerations in the design of your educational platform. Design choices, such as color schemes, imagery, and symbols, can have a significant impact on how your platform is perceived by users from different cultural backgrounds.

Cultural Sensitivity

Cultural sensitivity in design means being aware of and respectful toward the cultural values, norms, and preferences of your target audience. Here are some key considerations:

Color Symbolism

Colors can carry different meanings and associations in different cultures. For example, while white represents purity in many Western cultures, it symbolizes mourning in some Asian cultures. Research color symbolism in your target regions to make informed color choices.

<!—Example: Using culturally appropriate color schemes—>

<div class="alert alert-success" **role**="alert">

Your progress is looking great!

</div>

Imagery and Icons

Images and icons used on your platform should be culturally neutral or culturally relevant, depending on your audience. Avoid using symbols or images that may have negative connotations in certain cultures.

<!—Example: Using culturally relevant imagery—>

<img src="traditional_dance.jpg" **alt**="Traditional dance performance">

Language and Typography

Ensure that text is displayed in appropriate fonts and typography styles for each language and culture. Pay attention to text alignment, text direction (LTR or RTL), and font choices.

```
/* Example: CSS for Arabic text */

.arabic-text {

font-family: 'Amiri', serif;

direction: rtl;

}
```

Holidays and Events

Consider incorporating culturally significant holidays and events into your platform's design. This can foster a sense of belonging and engagement among users from specific cultural backgrounds.

User Feedback and Localization

Engage with users from different cultures to gather feedback on the platform's design. Conduct user testing with individuals who represent your diverse user base to identify any cultural issues or preferences.

Localization Beyond Language

Localization goes beyond language translation. It includes adapting content, design, and functionality to align with the cultural norms and expectations of your audience.

```
<!—Example: Displaying dates in a culturally appropriate format—>
```

```
<p>Date of Birth: {{ user.birthdate | date:'longDate' }}</p>
```

Accessibility for Diverse Users

Ensure that your design choices do not exclude users with disabilities from diverse cultural backgrounds. Test the accessibility of your platform for users with various needs.

User-Centric Design

Ultimately, a user-centric design approach is key to addressing cultural considerations. Be open to feedback, iterate on your design based on user preferences, and aim for an inclusive and culturally sensitive user experience.

Conclusion

Cultural considerations in design are crucial for creating a platform that resonates with a diverse user base. By being aware of color symbolism, using culturally relevant imagery and typography, considering holidays and events, engaging with users for feedback, and adopting a user-centric design approach, you can create a platform that welcomes and respects users from different cultural backgrounds. In the next section, we'll explore right-to-left (RTL) support and adaptation for languages that follow RTL text direction.

18.4 RTL Support and Adaptation

In this section, we'll delve into right-to-left (RTL) support and adaptation for languages that follow RTL text direction. Ensuring that your educational platform can effectively display and accommodate RTL languages is essential for reaching users from regions where RTL scripts are prevalent, such as Arabic, Hebrew, and Persian.

Understanding RTL Languages

RTL languages are written from right to left, which is the opposite direction of left-to-right (LTR) languages like English. This fundamental difference affects not only the text direction but also the layout, alignment, and behavior of various elements.

Enabling RTL Support

To enable RTL support in your Bootstrap-based platform, you can follow these steps:

1. HTML Direction Attribute

Apply the dir="rtl" attribute to the <html> tag in your HTML document to specify the overall text direction.

```
<!DOCTYPE html>

<html lang="ar" dir="rtl">

<!—...—>

</html>
```

2. CSS Adjustments

Adjust CSS styles to accommodate RTL layouts. For example, you may need to:

```
/* Example: CSS adjustments for RTL layouts */

body {
```

```
direction: rtl;

text-align: right;

}

/* Adjust margins and paddings */

.my-element {

margin-left: 10px; /* Margin on the right side for RTL */

}
```

3. RTL-Friendly Fonts

Select fonts that are designed to work well with RTL scripts, as some fonts may not render RTL characters correctly. Include these fonts in your CSS.

```
/* Example: Using a font that supports RTL scripts */

body {

font-family: 'Noto Sans Arabic', sans-serif;

}
```

4. Mirrored Layout

In some cases, you may need to mirror the layout of certain elements, such as navigation menus, to ensure their correct appearance in RTL languages.

```
<!—Example: Mirrored navigation menu for RTL support—>

<nav>
```

```
<ul class="rtl-menu">
<li><a href="#">الصفحة الرئيسية</a></li>
<li><a href="#">منتجات</a></li>
<!—Add more menu items—>
</ul>
</nav>
```

5. Text Direction Markup

Use appropriate HTML markup to specify text direction within individual elements, especially if you have mixed LTR and RTL content on the same page.

```
<!—Example: Specifying text direction within an element—>
<p>This is an LTR paragraph.</p>
<p dir="rtl">هذه فقرة RTL.</p>
```

Testing RTL Layouts

Thoroughly test your platform's RTL layouts by viewing pages in RTL languages. Verify that text flows correctly, alignment is consistent, and all elements are displayed as expected.

Content Localization

In addition to layout adjustments, ensure that your content is correctly localized for RTL languages. This includes text translations, date and time formats, and cultural considerations specific to RTL-speaking regions.

User Feedback

Engage with users who primarily use RTL languages to gather feedback on your platform's RTL support and usability. Their insights can help you make necessary improvements.

Conclusion

RTL support and adaptation are vital for accommodating users who interact with your educational platform in RTL languages. By implementing the steps mentioned above and ensuring that your content is correctly localized, you can create a seamless and user-friendly experience for RTL-speaking audiences. In the next section, we'll focus on testing your platform for a global audience.

18.5 Testing for Global Audiences

In this section, we'll explore the importance of thorough testing to ensure that your educational platform is well-suited for a global audience. Testing helps identify issues related to performance, localization, cultural sensitivity, and accessibility that may arise when catering to users from different regions and backgrounds.

Cross-Browser Compatibility

Ensure that your platform functions correctly across various web browsers. Test it on popular browsers such as Google Chrome, Mozilla Firefox, Microsoft Edge, Safari, and others to guarantee a consistent user experience.

```
<!—Example: Cross-browser testing—>

<!DOCTYPE html>

<html lang="en">
```

```
<head>
<meta charset="UTF-8">
<title>Platform Testing</title>
<!—Include Bootstrap and other CSS/JS resources—>
</head>
<body>
<!—Content of your platform—>
</body>
</html>
```

Responsive Design

Verify that your platform's responsive design adapts gracefully to different screen sizes and orientations. Test on a variety of devices, including desktops, laptops, tablets, and smartphones.

```
/* Example: Media query for responsive design testing */
@media (max-width: 768px) {
/* Styles for smaller screens */
}
```

Load Testing

Perform load testing to assess how your platform handles concurrent users. Identify and address performance bottlenecks to ensure a smooth experience, especially during peak usage times.

// Example: Load testing with a tool like Apache JMeter

Localization Testing

Test your platform with multiple languages, including RTL languages, to ensure that text, layouts, and content are properly localized. Verify that date and time formats, numeric representations, and cultural considerations align with the expectations of different regions.

Accessibility Testing

Conduct accessibility testing to ensure that your platform is usable by individuals with disabilities. Use assistive technologies and screen readers to identify and fix accessibility issues.

<!—Example: Testing with a screen reader—>

<audio src="audio.mp3" **controls>**

Your browser does not support the audio element.

</audio>

Cultural Sensitivity Testing

Review your platform's design and content for cultural sensitivity. Ensure that color choices, imagery, icons, and symbols are appropriate and respectful to users from diverse cultural backgrounds.

Performance Optimization

Optimize your platform's performance by minifying CSS and JavaScript, optimizing images, leveraging browser caching, and utilizing Content Delivery Networks (CDNs). Monitor performance regularly.

// Example: Minifying CSS and JavaScript

User Testing

Engage with users from various regions and backgrounds to gather feedback. Conduct usability testing to identify issues that may not be apparent through automated testing.

Global Audience Considerations

Remember that your platform may be accessed by users with different internet speeds, devices, and cultural expectations. Consider these factors when making design and functionality decisions.

Conclusion

Testing for a global audience is a critical step in ensuring that your educational platform provides a seamless and inclusive experience for users from diverse backgrounds. By addressing cross-browser compatibility, responsive design, load testing, localization, accessibility, cultural sensitivity, performance optimization, and gathering user feedback, you can create a platform that is accessible and valuable to learners worldwide. In the final chapter, we'll explore performance optimization techniques to further enhance your platform's efficiency and speed.

Chapter 19: Performance Optimization

19.1 Speeding Up Bootstrap Websites

In this section, we'll focus on speeding up your Bootstrap-based educational platform by implementing various performance optimization techniques. A fast-loading website not only enhances user experience but also positively impacts SEO rankings and user engagement.

Importance of Website Speed

Website speed is a critical factor that influences user satisfaction and retention. A slow website can lead to high bounce rates, lower conversion rates, and frustration among users. Therefore, optimizing your platform for speed is essential.

1. Minify CSS and JavaScript

Minifying CSS and JavaScript files involves removing unnecessary whitespace, comments, and formatting. This reduces file size and improves loading times.

```
<!—Example: Including minified CSS and JavaScript files—>

<link rel="stylesheet" href="styles.min.css">

<script src="scripts.min.js"></script>
```

2. Optimize Images

Large image files can significantly slow down your website. Use image optimization tools to compress images while maintaining quality.

<!—Example: Optimizing images for web—>

<**img** **src**="optimized-image.jpg" **alt**="Optimized Image">

3. Lazy Loading

Lazy loading defers the loading of images and other non-essential resources until they are needed. This can dramatically improve initial page load times.

<!—Example: Lazy loading images—>

<**img** **src**="placeholder.jpg" **data-src**="image-to-load.jpg" **alt**="Lazy Loaded Image" **loading**="lazy">

4. Browser Caching

Leverage browser caching by setting appropriate cache headers for your assets. This allows browsers to store resources locally, reducing the need to download them on subsequent visits.

Example: Setting cache headers in .htaccess (Apache)

<IfModule mod_expires.c>

ExpiresActive On

ExpiresByType image/jpg "access plus 1 year"

ExpiresByType image/jpeg "access plus 1 year"

ExpiresByType image/gif "access plus 1 year"

</IfModule>

5. Content Delivery Network (CDN)

A CDN can distribute your website's content across multiple servers worldwide. This reduces the distance between the user and the server, resulting in faster loading times.

```
<!—Example: Using a CDN for Bootstrap resources—>

<link rel="stylesheet" href="https://cdn.jsdelivr.net/npm/bootstrap@5.3.0/dist/css/bootstrap.min.css">

<script src="https://cdn.jsdelivr.net/npm/bootstrap@5.3.0/dist/js/bootstrap.min.js"></script>
```

6. Server-Side Optimization

Optimize your server-side code for efficiency. Use server caching, minimize database queries, and consider server upgrades or scaling for high traffic periods.

```
// Example: Implementing server-side caching in Node.js

const express = require('express');

const app = express();

const cacheMiddleware = (req, res, next) => {

// Check if the response is cached

// If cached, serve the cached response

// If not cached, proceed with the request and cache the response

};

app.get('/route', cacheMiddleware, (req, res) => {
```

```
// Your route logic here
});
```

7. Reduce HTTP Requests

Minimize the number of HTTP requests required to load a page. Combine and bundle CSS and JavaScript files to reduce the number of separate requests.

```
<!—Example: Combining and bundling CSS and JavaScript—>
<link rel="stylesheet" href="styles.min.css">
<script src="scripts.min.js"></script>
```

8. Mobile Optimization

Ensure that your platform is optimized for mobile devices. Use responsive design techniques to adapt the layout for smaller screens.

```
/* Example: Media query for mobile optimization */
@media (max-width: 768px) {
/* Styles for smaller screens */
}
```

9. Performance Monitoring

Regularly monitor your website's performance using tools like Google PageSpeed Insights, GTmetrix, or WebPageTest. Identify and address any performance bottlenecks.

10. Content Delivery Optimization

Optimize the delivery of dynamic content. Use content delivery networks (CDNs) for caching and content distribution, and employ server-side techniques like caching and load balancing.

Conclusion

Speeding up your Bootstrap-based educational platform is crucial for providing a better user experience and achieving higher search engine rankings. By implementing techniques such as minifying CSS and JavaScript, optimizing images, lazy loading, browser caching, using CDNs, server-side optimization, reducing HTTP requests, mobile optimization, performance monitoring, and content delivery optimization, you can create a faster and more efficient platform. In the final chapter, we'll explore the future of Bootstrap and the importance of ongoing education and resources.

19.2 Optimizing Images and Media

In this section, we'll delve into optimizing images and media assets on your Bootstrap-based educational platform. Efficiently managing and serving images and media can significantly improve page load times and user experience.

Importance of Image Optimization

Images and media files often constitute a significant portion of a web page's size. Optimizing them reduces bandwidth usage, decreases load times, and benefits users with slower internet connections or limited data plans.

1. Choose the Right Image Format

Select the appropriate image format for each use case:

- **JPEG (Joint Photographic Experts Group):** Suitable for photographs and images with gradients. Use compression settings to balance quality and file size.

```html
<!—Example: Using a JPEG image—>

<img src="photo.jpg" alt="Photograph" />
```

- **PNG (Portable Network Graphics):** Ideal for images with transparency, logos, and graphics. Use PNG-8 for simple graphics and PNG-24 for images with transparency.

```html
<!—Example: Using a PNG image with transparency—>

<img src="logo.png" alt="Logo" />
```

- **SVG (Scalable Vector Graphics):** Perfect for logos and icons as they can scale without loss of quality.

```html
<!—Example: Using an SVG icon—>

<svg xmlns="http://www.w3.org/2000/svg" width="100" height="100" viewBox="0 0 100 100">

<circle cx="50" cy="50" r="40" fill="blue" />

</svg>
```

2. Resize and Compress Images

Use image editing software to resize images to their displayed dimensions on the website. Additionally, compress images to reduce file sizes while maintaining acceptable quality.

3. Implement Lazy Loading

Implement lazy loading for images and videos, which ensures that media assets are loaded only when they are in the user's viewport.

```
<!—Example: Lazy loading an image—>

<img src="placeholder.jpg" data-src="image-to-load.jpg" alt="Lazy Loaded Image" loading="lazy" />
```

4. Serve Images via CDNs

Consider serving images from Content Delivery Networks (CDNs) to take advantage of their global distribution and efficient delivery.

5. Use WebP Format (Optional)

WebP is a modern image format that provides excellent compression and quality. Use it for browsers that support it to further optimize image loading.

```
<!—Example: Using WebP format for modern browsers—>

<picture>

<source srcset="image.webp" type="image/webp">

<img src="fallback.jpg" alt="Image">

</picture>
```

6. Enable Image Compression

Configure server-side image compression to further reduce image file sizes.

```
# Example: Enabling image compression in .htaccess (Apache)

<IfModule mod_deflate.c>

AddOutputFilterByType DEFLATE image/jpeg image/png image/webp

</IfModule>
```

7. Lazy Load Videos

For videos, consider lazy loading techniques or using third-party services like YouTube or Vimeo, which optimize video delivery.

```
<!—Example: Embedding a YouTube video with lazy loading—>

<iframe

width="560"

height="315"

src="https://www.youtube.com/embed/VIDEO_ID"

frameborder="0"

allow="accelerometer; autoplay; clipboard-write; encrypted-media; gyroscope; picture-in-picture"

allowfullscreen

loading="lazy"

></iframe>
```

8. Optimize Audio Files

For audio files, use formats like MP3 with efficient compression settings. Additionally, consider audio streaming services for large audio libraries.

9. Reduce Multimedia Elements

Evaluate whether certain multimedia elements, such as heavy animations or auto-playing videos, are necessary. Minimize their usage to improve performance.

10. Monitor and Update

Regularly monitor your platform's media assets and update them as needed. Remove unused or outdated media files to keep your website lightweight.

Conclusion

Optimizing images and media assets is a crucial step in improving the performance of your Bootstrap-based educational platform. By selecting the right image format, resizing and compressing images, implementing lazy loading, serving images via CDNs, using the WebP format, enabling image compression, lazy loading videos, optimizing audio files, reducing multimedia elements, and regularly monitoring and updating media assets, you can enhance page load times and provide a faster and more responsive user experience. In the next section, we'll explore additional techniques such as minifying CSS and JavaScript to further boost your platform's performance.

19.3 Minifying CSS and JavaScript

In this section, we'll delve into the practice of minifying CSS and JavaScript files to improve the performance of your Bootstrap-based educational platform. Minification involves the removal of unnecessary characters and whitespace from code files, resulting in smaller file sizes that load faster in users' browsers.

The Importance of Minification

Minifying CSS and JavaScript files is crucial for reducing the amount of data that needs to be transferred over the internet when a user visits your website. Smaller files lead to quicker loading times, which, in turn, improves the overall user experience.

CSS Minification

To minify CSS files, you can follow these steps:

1. Use a CSS minification tool: Several online tools and build tools (like Grunt, Gulp, or Webpack) can automatically minify your CSS files during the build process.
2. Manual minification: If you prefer manual control, you can use online CSS minifiers or text editors with built-in minification features. Remove comments, unnecessary whitespace, and line breaks to reduce file size.

/ Original CSS with comments */*

body {

background-color: #f0f0f0;

/ Set font size to 16 pixels */*

```
font-size: 16px;

}

/* Minified CSS */

body{background-color:#f0f0f0;font-size:16px;}
```

1. Utilize minified CSS libraries: If you're using Bootstrap or other CSS frameworks, consider using their minified versions, which are already optimized for size and performance.

JavaScript Minification

Minifying JavaScript files is essential for efficient loading. Here's how to minify JavaScript:

1. Use a JavaScript minification tool: Just like with CSS, you can use various online tools or build tools to minify your JavaScript files automatically.
2. Manual minification: If you prefer manual minification, remove comments, whitespace, and unnecessary line breaks from your JavaScript code.

```
/* Original JavaScript with comments */

function greet(name) {

// Display a greeting message

console.log('Hello, ' + name + '!');

}

/* Minified JavaScript */
```

```
function greet(e){console.log('Hello, '+e+'!');}
```

1. Employ a JavaScript bundler: Tools like Webpack or Parcel can bundle and minify multiple JavaScript files into a single minified file, reducing HTTP requests and improving performance.

Combining Minified Files

To further optimize your platform's performance, combine multiple minified CSS and JavaScript files into a single file. This reduces the number of HTTP requests required to load your site.

```
<!—Example: Combining and serving minified CSS and JavaScript—>

<link rel="stylesheet" href="combined.min.css">

<script src="combined.min.js"></script>
```

Gzipping Minified Files

Consider enabling Gzip compression on your web server to further reduce the size of minified files during transmission. Most modern web servers support Gzip compression.

```
# Example: Enabling Gzip compression in .htaccess (Apache)

<IfModule mod_deflate.c>

AddOutputFilterByType DEFLATE text/css text/javascript application/javascript

</IfModule>
```

Regular Maintenance

Regularly update and maintain your minified CSS and JavaScript files as you make changes to your platform. Ensure that you keep the minified versions up to date.

Conclusion

Minifying CSS and JavaScript is a fundamental practice for improving the performance of your Bootstrap-based educational platform. By reducing the size of these files through minification, combining minified files, enabling Gzip compression, and maintaining the minified versions, you can significantly enhance the loading speed of your platform, resulting in a better user experience. In the next section, we'll explore leveraging browser caching and optimizing server-side performance to further boost your platform's speed and responsiveness.

19.4 Leveraging Browser Caching

In this section, we'll delve into the practice of leveraging browser caching to enhance the performance of your Bootstrap-based educational platform. Browser caching allows you to store certain website assets locally on users' devices, reducing load times for subsequent visits.

The Importance of Browser Caching

Browser caching is essential for improving the loading speed of your platform, especially for returning visitors. When users access your site multiple times, their browsers can retrieve cached resources instead of downloading them again, resulting in faster page loads.

Setting Cache-Control Headers

To implement browser caching, you need to set appropriate Cache-Control headers for your assets on the server. These headers instruct browsers how to handle caching for specific resources.

Here's how you can set cache headers in different server environments:

Apache (in .htaccess)

For an Apache web server, you can use the following directives in your .htaccess file to set cache headers:

```
# Cache images and media files for one year

<IfModule mod_expires.c>

ExpiresActive On

ExpiresByType image/jpeg "access plus 1 year"

ExpiresByType image/png "access plus 1 year"

ExpiresByType image/gif "access plus 1 year"

</IfModule>
```

Nginx (in nginx.conf)

If you're using Nginx, you can configure cache headers in your server block as follows:

```
location ~* \.(jpg|jpeg|png|gif)$ {

expires 365d;
```

```
}
```

PHP (in .php files)

In PHP, you can set cache headers directly in your server-side code:

```
<?php
// Cache images and media files for one year
$expires = 60 * 60 * 24 * 365; // 1 year in seconds
header("Cache-Control: public, max-age=$expires");
```

Cache-Control Directives

The Cache-Control header uses various directives to control caching behavior. Here are some common directives:

- public: Indicates that the resource can be cached by both the browser and intermediate caches (e.g., CDNs).
- private: Specifies that the resource is specific to the user and should not be cached by shared caches.
- max-age: Defines the maximum time (in seconds) the resource can be cached. For example, max-age=3600 caches the resource for one hour.
- s-maxage: Similar to max-age, but applies only to shared caches (e.g., CDNs).

Cache Busting

While browser caching is beneficial, it can sometimes lead to issues when you update your assets. To overcome this, use cache busting techniques, such as appending a version number or timestamp to your asset URLs.

```
<!—Example: Cache busting with a version number—>

<link rel="stylesheet" href="styles.css?v=1.0">

<script src="scripts.js?v=1.0"></script>
```

By changing the version number (e.g., from 1.0 to 2.0) when you update your assets, you ensure that browsers fetch the latest versions.

Browser Cache Testing

After implementing browser caching, thoroughly test your platform to verify that cached assets are served correctly and that changes to assets trigger cache invalidation.

Conclusion

Leveraging browser caching is a fundamental practice for improving the performance and load times of your Bootstrap-based educational platform. By setting Cache-Control headers, understanding cache directives, implementing cache busting techniques, and regularly testing caching behavior, you can ensure that your platform provides a fast and responsive user experience for both first-time visitors and returning users. In the next section, we'll explore the use of Content Delivery Networks (CDNs) and server-side considerations for further performance optimization.

19.5 CDN and Server-side Considerations

In this section, we'll explore the use of Content Delivery Networks (CDNs) and server-side considerations to further optimize the performance of your Bootstrap-based educational platform. CDNs and server-side optimizations play a crucial role in delivering content quickly and efficiently to users.

Content Delivery Networks (CDNs)

A CDN is a distributed network of servers strategically located around the world. CDNs store cached copies of your website's assets, such as images, scripts, and stylesheets, on these servers. When a user requests content from your website, the CDN serves it from the nearest server, reducing latency and load times. Here's how to utilize CDNs effectively:

1. **Choose a CDN Provider:** Select a reputable CDN provider like Amazon CloudFront, Cloudflare, or Akamai. Consider your budget, geographic reach, and the types of content you need to deliver.
2. **Integrate Bootstrap via CDN:** Bootstrap offers CDN-hosted versions of its library, allowing you to load it directly from the CDN's servers.

```
<!—Example: Loading Bootstrap via CDN—>

<link rel="stylesheet" href="https://cdn.jsdelivr.net/npm/bootstrap@5.3.0/dist/css/bootstrap.min.css">

<script src="https://cdn.jsdelivr.net/npm/bootstrap@5.3.0/dist/js/bootstrap.min.js"></script>
```

1. **Optimize CDN Caching:** Configure cache settings for your assets in the CDN dashboard. Specify cache lifetimes based on asset volatility. For static assets like images, longer cache durations are suitable, while dynamic content should have shorter cache durations.
2. **Content Purging:** Ensure that your CDN allows you to

purge or invalidate cached content when updates are made to your website. This ensures that users always receive the latest content.

Server-side Considerations

Optimizing your server-side code and infrastructure is equally important for performance. Here are some server-side considerations:

1. **Server Caching:** Implement server-side caching mechanisms to reduce the load on your server and improve response times. Common caching methods include Redis, Memcached, and object caching in PHP.
2. **Database Optimization:** Optimize your database queries and indexes to reduce query execution times. Use query caching and consider database replication for high-traffic websites.
3. **Content Compression:** Enable Gzip or Brotli compression on your web server to reduce the size of assets before sending them to users' browsers.
4. **Load Balancing:** Distribute incoming traffic across multiple server instances to ensure that your platform can handle high loads. Consider using load balancing services or technologies like Docker Swarm or Kubernetes.
5. **Content Security Policies (CSP):** Implement CSP headers to mitigate security risks, but be mindful of their impact on performance. Ensure that your CSP settings allow the loading of assets from trusted sources.
6. **Server Scaling:** Be prepared to scale your server infrastructure as your platform grows. Cloud services like AWS, Google Cloud, and Azure offer auto-scaling capabilities.

7. **Content Preloading:** Use the preload directive in your HTML to instruct browsers to fetch critical resources early in the loading process.

```
<!—Example: Preloading a CSS file—>

<link rel="preload" href="styles.css" as="style" onload="this.onload=null;this.rel='stylesheet'">

<noscript><link rel="stylesheet" href="styles.css"></noscript>
```

1. **Monitoring and Optimization:** Regularly monitor your server's performance using tools like New Relic, Datadog, or built-in server monitoring tools. Identify bottlenecks and optimize server configurations accordingly.

Testing and Performance Analysis

Perform regular testing and performance analysis using tools like Google PageSpeed Insights, GTmetrix, and WebPageTest. These tools can help you identify performance bottlenecks and fine-tune your CDN and server-side optimizations.

Conclusion

Utilizing Content Delivery Networks (CDNs) and implementing server-side considerations are crucial steps in optimizing the performance of your Bootstrap-based educational platform. CDNs help deliver content quickly to users by distributing it across a global network of servers, while server-side optimizations ensure that your platform can handle traffic efficiently. By choosing the right CDN provider, integrating Bootstrap via CDN, optimizing CDN caching, configuring content purging, and addressing server-side aspects like caching, database optimization, content compression, load balancing, security policies, scaling, content preloading, and monitoring, you can provide a fast and reliable user experience. In the final chapter, we'll discuss the future of Bootstrap and the importance of ongoing education and resources for staying up to date with performance optimization techniques.

20.1 Upcoming Features and Updates

In this final chapter, we'll explore the future of Bootstrap and the exciting features and updates that lie ahead. As web development technologies continue to evolve, Bootstrap aims to stay at the forefront by introducing new capabilities and improvements.

Bootstrap 6

Bootstrap 6 is on the horizon, and it promises to bring a host of enhancements and modernizations to the framework. While specific details may change, here are some areas where Bootstrap 6 is likely to focus:

1. **Modern CSS:** Bootstrap 6 may transition to modern CSS features, such as CSS Grid and custom properties (CSS variables), to provide more flexibility in layout and design.
2. **Improved Responsiveness:** Expect further improvements in responsive design to adapt to an even wider range of devices and screen sizes.
3. **Web Component Integration:** Bootstrap may explore better integration with web components, allowing for more modular and reusable UI elements.
4. **Accessibility:** Enhancing accessibility features will continue to be a priority, ensuring that Bootstrap remains inclusive and usable by all.
5. **Performance:** Bootstrap 6 may include optimizations to

further improve performance, including smaller file sizes and faster load times.

6. **JavaScript Frameworks:** The framework may offer better integration with popular JavaScript frameworks like React, Vue.js, and Angular.

Community Contributions

Bootstrap thrives on its vibrant open-source community. Contributors from around the world play a significant role in shaping the framework's direction. As Bootstrap 6 development progresses, community involvement is likely to remain a driving force.

Ongoing Education and Resources

To stay up to date with Bootstrap's latest features and updates, it's essential to engage in ongoing education and access valuable resources. Here are some ways to do so:

1. **Official Documentation:** Continuously refer to the official Bootstrap documentation for the latest information on components, utilities, and best practices.
2. **GitHub Repository:** Follow the Bootstrap GitHub repository to track issues, contribute code, and stay informed about development progress.
3. **Community Forums:** Join online forums and communities related to Bootstrap, such as Stack Overflow or the Bootstrap Discord server, to ask questions and share knowledge.
4. **Tutorials and Blogs:** Explore tutorials and blogs from web development experts who share insights, tips, and tricks related to Bootstrap.

5. **Online Courses:** Enroll in online courses and tutorials dedicated to Bootstrap to deepen your understanding and proficiency.
6. **Webinars and Conferences:** Attend webinars, conferences, and workshops focused on web development and Bootstrap to gain insights from industry experts.

Conclusion

As Bootstrap continues to evolve, web developers can look forward to Bootstrap 6 and its promising features and updates. Embracing the framework's improvements and staying connected with the Bootstrap community and educational resources will empower you to create responsive and feature-rich web applications that meet the demands of modern web development. Whether you're building an educational platform, an eCommerce website, or any other web project, Bootstrap remains a valuable tool for achieving your design and performance goals. Thank you for joining us on this Bootstrap journey, and we wish you success in your web development endeavors!

20.2 The Role of Bootstrap in Modern Web Design

Bootstrap has played a significant role in shaping modern web design practices and standards. Since its initial release, it has consistently been a popular choice among developers for creating responsive and visually appealing websites. In this section, we'll explore the role of Bootstrap in modern web design and how it has influenced the way we approach web development.

Responsive Web Design

One of Bootstrap's most prominent contributions to modern web design is its emphasis on responsive design principles. Bootstrap was one of the early frameworks to promote the idea that websites should adapt seamlessly to different screen sizes and devices. By utilizing a grid system, responsive utilities, and responsive breakpoints, Bootstrap made it easier for developers to create websites that look and function well on desktops, tablets, and smartphones. This focus on responsive design has become a standard practice in the web development industry.

Faster Development and Prototyping

Bootstrap introduced a comprehensive set of pre-designed components and UI elements that developers can readily use. These components include navigation bars, forms, modals, carousels, and more. By leveraging these ready-made components, developers can significantly accelerate the development process, reduce code duplication, and quickly prototype web interfaces. This speed and efficiency are particularly valuable in today's fast-paced web development landscape.

Consistency and Branding

Bootstrap's consistent and well-designed components provide a foundation for maintaining brand consistency across a website. Designers and developers can customize Bootstrap's default styles to match a brand's visual identity, ensuring that every part of the website adheres to the same design standards. This level of consistency helps reinforce brand recognition and trust among users.

Accessibility and Inclusivity

Accessibility is a fundamental consideration in modern web design, and Bootstrap has made strides in this area. It includes accessibility features and best practices to ensure that websites built with Bootstrap are usable by individuals with disabilities. This commitment to inclusivity aligns with evolving web accessibility standards and regulations, such as WCAG (Web Content Accessibility Guidelines).

Integration with JavaScript Frameworks

As the web development landscape has evolved, so has Bootstrap's compatibility with various JavaScript frameworks and libraries. Developers can seamlessly integrate Bootstrap with popular frameworks like React, Angular, and Vue.js. This flexibility allows them to leverage the power of Bootstrap's UI components while building dynamic and interactive web applications.

Collaboration and Community

Bootstrap's open-source nature has fostered a thriving community of developers, designers, and contributors. Collaboration and the sharing of knowledge have become integral to modern web design practices. Developers can tap into community resources, engage in discussions, and access third-party plugins and extensions that enhance Bootstrap's capabilities.

Future-Proofing and Adaptation

Bootstrap's commitment to staying current with web development trends and technologies ensures that it remains a relevant and adaptable tool. Its upcoming releases, such as Bootstrap 6, promise to bring modern CSS features, improved responsiveness, and better integration with evolving web technologies. This dedication to evolution and innovation positions Bootstrap as a future-proof choice for web designers and developers.

In conclusion, Bootstrap has played a pivotal role in modern web design by promoting responsive design, accelerating development, ensuring consistency, prioritizing accessibility, and adapting to the ever-changing web development landscape. As web technologies continue to advance, Bootstrap is poised to remain a valuable tool for creating exceptional web experiences. Whether you're a seasoned web developer or just starting your journey, Bootstrap's influence on modern web design is undeniable, and it continues to shape the way we build and design websites.

20.3 Community Contributions and Open Source

The success of Bootstrap as a widely adopted and influential web framework can be attributed in large part to its open-source nature and the active contributions of the web development community. In this section, we'll delve into the significance of community contributions and open source in the Bootstrap project and explore how they have shaped its development.

Open Source Philosophy

Bootstrap was initially created by Twitter engineers Mark Otto and Jacob Thornton as an internal project. Recognizing its potential to benefit the wider web development community, they decided to release it as an open-source project under the MIT license. This decision to embrace open source was pivotal, as it allowed developers worldwide to access, use, modify, and contribute to Bootstrap freely.

Collaborative Development

Bootstrap's development has always been a collaborative effort. A diverse group of developers from different backgrounds and regions has come together to improve and expand the framework. This collaborative approach has accelerated the pace of development and ensured that Bootstrap remains relevant and up-to-date with modern web development practices.

GitHub and Version Control

Bootstrap's codebase is hosted on GitHub, one of the world's largest platforms for open-source collaboration. GitHub provides version control, issue tracking, and collaboration tools that make it easy for developers to work together. The platform also enables transparent communication between contributors and users, fostering a sense of community and accountability.

Issue Reporting and Resolution

The Bootstrap GitHub repository serves as a central hub for issue reporting and resolution. Developers and users can submit bug reports, feature requests, and code contributions through the platform. This open and transparent process allows issues to be addressed promptly and ensures that Bootstrap continues to improve.

Third-Party Plugins and Extensions

Bootstrap's open-source ecosystem extends beyond the core framework. A wide range of third-party plugins and extensions has been developed by the community to enhance Bootstrap's functionality. These plugins cover everything from additional UI components to integrations with other JavaScript libraries and frameworks. This ecosystem provides developers with a rich set of tools to extend Bootstrap's capabilities.

Documentation and Localization

The Bootstrap documentation, available in multiple languages, is another area where community contributions shine. Contributors have translated the documentation to make it accessible to a global audience. Additionally, community members have written tutorials, guides, and documentation enhancements to help users understand and leverage Bootstrap effectively.

Empowering Developers

Open source projects like Bootstrap empower developers to take control of their web development projects. By contributing to the project, developers can have a direct impact on the evolution of the framework and help shape its future. This sense of ownership and involvement in an open-source community is a driving force behind the success of Bootstrap.

Learning and Mentorship

Participating in the Bootstrap community offers valuable learning opportunities and mentorship. Novice developers can learn from experienced contributors, gain exposure to best practices, and enhance their skills. This collaborative environment fosters knowledge sharing and skill development, benefiting developers at all levels of expertise.

Community Engagement

Bootstrap's community engagement extends beyond code contributions. The Bootstrap community actively participates in discussions, forums, and social media platforms to exchange ideas, troubleshoot issues, and share insights. This sense of camaraderie and support strengthens the bond among developers.

In conclusion, Bootstrap's thriving open-source community is a testament to the power of collaboration and the collective effort of web developers worldwide. This community-driven approach has enabled Bootstrap to remain at the forefront of modern web development, continually adapting to meet the evolving needs of web designers and developers. Whether you're a seasoned contributor or a newcomer, Bootstrap's open-source philosophy invites you to be a part of its ongoing success and to shape the future of web development. Open source has played a vital role in Bootstrap's journey, and it continues to be a source of inspiration and innovation for web developers worldwide.

20.4 Preparing for Bootstrap 6

As Bootstrap continues to evolve and adapt to the changing landscape of web development, it's essential for developers and organizations to prepare for Bootstrap 6 and embrace the upcoming changes and improvements. In this section, we'll explore how you can get ready for Bootstrap 6 and ensure a smooth transition when it becomes available.

Stay Informed

To prepare for Bootstrap 6, it's crucial to stay informed about the latest developments and announcements regarding the new version. Keep an eye on the official Bootstrap website, blog, and GitHub repository for updates and release notes. Following Bootstrap's official social media accounts and subscribing to newsletters can also help you stay up to date with important news and timelines.

Review Documentation

Familiarize yourself with Bootstrap's official documentation, especially any documentation related to version changes and migration guides. Bootstrap's documentation typically provides detailed information on what's new, deprecated, or modified in each release. Reviewing these documents can help you understand the changes you'll need to make to your projects.

Assess Impact on Existing Projects

If you have existing projects built with Bootstrap, assess the impact of migrating to Bootstrap 6. Consider factors like compatibility, deprecated features, and the effort required to update your codebase. It's a good practice to create a checklist of changes needed for each project.

Update Dependencies

Ensure that any third-party dependencies or plugins you rely on in your Bootstrap projects are compatible with Bootstrap 6. Some plugins and extensions may require updates to align with the new version. Check the documentation and repositories of these dependencies for information on compatibility and updates.

Test and Debug

Before fully migrating to Bootstrap 6, set up a testing environment where you can experiment with the new version without affecting your production code. Test your projects thoroughly to identify any issues, bugs, or compatibility issues. Debug and address these issues in your test environment before migrating your live projects.

Plan for Compatibility

Bootstrap 6 may introduce breaking changes, which means that some of your existing code may no longer work as expected. Plan for these compatibility issues by identifying the parts of your codebase that may be affected. Make necessary adjustments and updates to ensure that your projects continue to function correctly.

Explore New Features

Bootstrap 6 is likely to bring new features, improvements, and enhancements. Take the time to explore these additions and understand how they can benefit your projects. Familiarize yourself with any new components, utilities, or design patterns introduced in Bootstrap 6.

Consider Performance

As Bootstrap evolves, it often includes optimizations for performance. Evaluate the performance of your projects with Bootstrap 6 to ensure that they benefit from any performance enhancements. Look for opportunities to optimize your code further and improve load times.

Plan Training and Education

If you work in a team or organization, plan for training and education related to Bootstrap 6. Ensure that team members are aware of the upcoming changes and are prepared to work with the new version effectively. Training sessions, workshops, or online courses may be beneficial.

Engage with the Community

Engage with the Bootstrap community and participate in discussions related to Bootstrap 6. Share your experiences, ask questions, and seek advice from other developers who are also preparing for the transition. Community insights and support can be valuable during the migration process.

In conclusion, preparing for Bootstrap 6 involves staying informed, reviewing documentation, assessing the impact on existing projects, updating dependencies, thorough testing, planning for compatibility, exploring new features, considering performance improvements, planning for training, and engaging with the community. Bootstrap 6 promises to bring exciting changes and enhancements to the framework, and by proactively preparing for its release, you can ensure a seamless transition and continue to leverage Bootstrap's capabilities for your web development projects. Keep an eye on Bootstrap's official channels for updates, and when the time comes, embrace Bootstrap 6 to stay at the forefront of modern web design and development.

20.5 Continuing Education and Resources

Web development is an ever-evolving field, and staying up to date with the latest trends, technologies, and best practices is essential for web developers and designers. In this final section, we'll explore the importance of continuing education and provide a list of resources to help you further your knowledge and skills in Bootstrap and web development.

Lifelong Learning

Lifelong learning is a fundamental aspect of a successful career in web development. As technologies and tools evolve, it's crucial to invest time and effort into expanding your knowledge and skills. Continuing education ensures that you can adapt to new challenges and take advantage of emerging opportunities in the field.

Online Courses and Tutorials

Online courses and tutorials are excellent resources for learning and improving your Bootstrap skills. Websites like Coursera, Udemy, edX, and Codecademy offer a wide range of courses on Bootstrap and web development. These courses cover various topics, from the basics of Bootstrap to advanced techniques and best practices.

Documentation and Official Resources

Bootstrap's official documentation is a comprehensive resource for understanding the framework's components, utilities, and features. Regularly refer to the official documentation to stay informed about the latest updates and recommended practices. Additionally, Bootstrap's official website and blog provide valuable insights and announcements.

Books and Ebooks

Numerous books and ebooks are dedicated to Bootstrap and web development. These resources offer in-depth explanations, practical examples, and guidance for mastering Bootstrap. Look for titles like "Bootstrap 5 Handbook" and "Mastering Bootstrap 4" to expand your knowledge.

Web Development Blogs

Many web development blogs and websites regularly publish articles, tutorials, and tips related to Bootstrap and web design. Follow popular blogs such as Smashing Magazine, CSS-Tricks, and A List Apart to stay informed about industry trends and best practices.

Webinars and Conferences

Webinars and conferences offer opportunities to learn from industry experts, gain insights into the latest web development trends, and network with fellow professionals. Keep an eye out for webinars and conferences focused on Bootstrap and web design, and consider attending or watching recorded sessions.

Online Communities and Forums

Online communities and forums are valuable platforms for asking questions, seeking advice, and sharing knowledge with other web developers. Websites like Stack Overflow, Reddit's web development subreddits, and the Bootstrap Discord server are excellent places to engage with the community.

GitHub Repositories

Explore GitHub repositories related to Bootstrap to discover open-source projects, plugins, and extensions created by the community. Contributing to open-source projects can be an educational and rewarding experience.

Code Challenges and Practice

Regularly practice your Bootstrap skills by taking on coding challenges and projects. Websites like LeetCode, HackerRank, and freeCodeCamp offer coding challenges and projects that can help you refine your skills and problem-solving abilities.

Online Design and Development Tools

Experiment with online design and development tools that complement Bootstrap. Tools like Figma, Sketch, and CodePen can enhance your design and prototyping capabilities, allowing you to create responsive and visually appealing web interfaces.

Professional Networking

Building a professional network in the web development industry can open doors to opportunities, collaborations, and mentorship. Attend local meetups, join LinkedIn groups, and connect with professionals in your field.

In conclusion, continuing education is a vital aspect of a successful career in web development. By staying informed, regularly practicing your skills, and engaging with the web development community, you can ensure that you remain a proficient and adaptable developer. Bootstrap, with its ever-evolving features and capabilities, is an excellent tool to have in your web development toolkit. Utilize the resources mentioned above to continue your education, refine your skills, and excel in the dynamic world of web development. Remember that learning is a lifelong journey, and your commitment to education will contribute to your success in the field.

www.ingramcontent.com/pod-product-compliance
Lightning Source LLC
LaVergne TN
LVHW101612210926
848480LV00008B/49
* 9 7 9 8 2 2 3 6 1 8 3 6 2 *